Microsoft® Office Outlook® 2007

ILLUSTRATED

ESSENTIALS

Rachel Biheller Bunin

COURSE TECHNOLOGY
CENGAGE Learning

Australia • Brazil • Japan • Korea • Mexico • Singapore • Spain • United Kingdom • United States

COURSE TECHNOLOGY
CENGAGE Learning™

Microsoft® Office Outlook® 2007—Illustrated Essentials

Rachel Biheller Bunin

Senior Acquisitions Editor: Marjorie Hunt

Senior Product Manager: Christina Kling Garrett

Associate Product Manager: Rebecca Padrick

Editorial Assistant: Michelle Camisa

Marketing Coordinator: Jennifer Hankin

Developmental Editors: Pamela Conrad,
  Jeanne Herring

Production Editor: Catherine G. DiMassa

Copy Editor: Gary Michael Spahl

Proofreader: Kathy Orrino

Indexer: Alexandra Nickerson

QA Manuscript Reviewer: Serge Palladino

Cover Designers: Elizabeth Paquin, Kathleen Fivel

Cover Artist: Mark Hunt

Composition: GEX Publishing Services

For product information and technology assistance, contact us at
Cengage Learning Customer & Sales Support, 1-800-354-9706

For permission to use material from this text or product, submit all requests online at **cengage.com/permissions**
Further permissions questions can be emailed to
permissionrequest@cengage.com

ISBN-13: 978-1-4239-2567-5

ISBN-10: 1-4239-2567-X

Course Technology
25 Thomson Place
Boston, Massachusetts 02210
USA

Cengage Learning is a leading provider of customized learning solutions with office locations around the globe, including Singapore, the United Kingdom, Australia, Mexico, Brazil, and Japan. Locate your local office at:
international.cengage.com/region

Cengage Learning products are represented in Canada by Nelson Education, Ltd.

For your lifelong learning solutions, visit **course.cengage.com**

Purchase any of our products at your local college store or at our preferred online store **www.ichapters.com**

Printed in the United States of America
2 3 4 5 6 7 8 9 11 10 09 08

Contents

Preface

Welcome to *Microsoft Office Outlook 2007— Illustrated Essentials*. If this is your first experience with the Illustrated series, you'll see that this book has a unique design: each skill is presented on two facing pages, with steps on the left and screens on the right. The layout makes it easy to digest a skill without having to read a lot of text and flip pages to see an illustration.

This book is an ideal learning tool for a wide range of learners—the rookies will find the clean design easy to follow and focused with only essential information presented, and the hotshots will appreciate being able to move quickly through the lessons to find the information they need without reading a lot of text. The design also makes this a great reference after the course is over! See the illustration on the right to learn more about the pedagogical and design elements of a typical lesson.

What's New in This Edition

We've made many changes and enhancements to this edition to make it the best ever. Here are some highlights of what's new:

- **New Getting Started with Microsoft Office 2007 Unit**—This unit begins the book and gets students up to speed on features of Office 2007 that are common to all the applications, such as the Ribbon, the Office button, and the Quick Access toolbar.

- **New Case Study**—A new case study featuring Quest Specialty Travel provides a practical and fun scenario that students can relate to as they learn skills. This fictional company offers a wide variety of tours around the world.

Each two-page spread focuses on a single skill.

Concise text introduces the basic principles in the lesson and integrates a real-world case study.

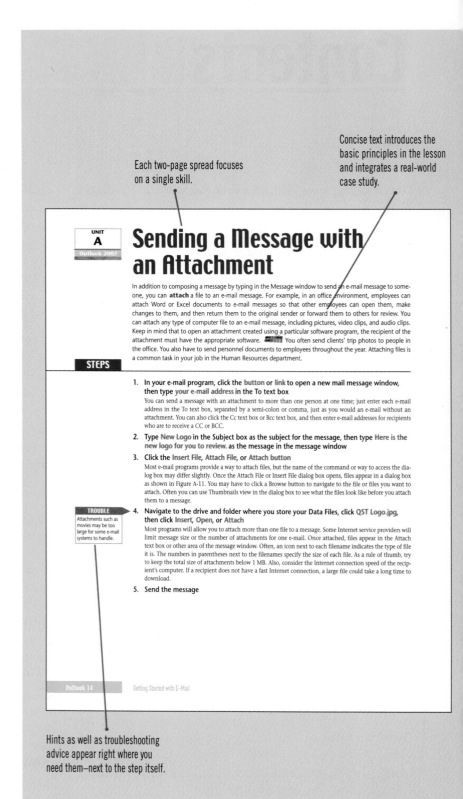

Hints as well as troubleshooting advice appear right where you need them—next to the step itself.

Every lesson features large, full-color representations of what the screen should look like as students complete the numbered steps.

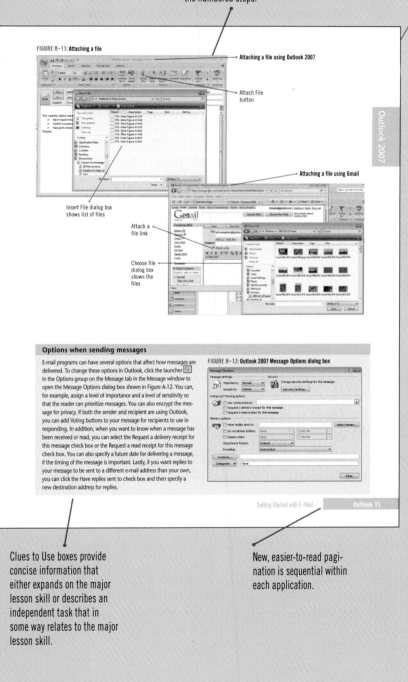

FIGURE A-11: Attaching a file

Attaching a file using Outlook 2007

Attach File button

Insert File dialog box shows list of files

Attach a file link

Choose file dialog box shows the files

Attaching a file using Gmail

Options when sending messages

E-mail programs can have several options that affect how messages are delivered. To change these options in Outlook, click the launcher in the Options group on the Message tab in the Message window to open the Message Options dialog box shown in Figure A-12. You can, for example, assign a level of importance and a level of sensitivity so that the reader can prioritize messages. You can also encrypt the message for privacy. If both the sender and recipient are using Outlook, you can add Voting buttons to your message for recipients to use in responding. In addition, when you want to know when a message has been received or read, you can select the Request a delivery receipt for this message check box or the Request a read receipt for this message check box. You can also specify a future date for delivering a message, if the timing of the message is important. Lastly, if you want replies to your message to be sent to a different e-mail address than your own, you can click the Have replies sent to check box and then specify a new destination address for replies.

FIGURE A-12: Outlook 2007 Message Options dialog box

Clues to Use boxes provide concise information that either expands on the major lesson skill or describes an independent task that in some way relates to the major lesson skill.

New, easier-to-read pagination is sequential within each application.

Assignments

The lessons use Quest Specialty Travel, a fictional adventure travel company, as the case study. The assignments on the light purple pages at the end of each unit increase in difficulty. Data files and case studies provide a variety of interesting and relevant business applications. Assignments include:

- **Concepts Reviews** consist of multiple choice, matching, and screen identification questions.
- **Skills Reviews** provide additional hands-on, step-by-step reinforcement.
- **Independent Challenges** are case projects requiring critical thinking and application of the unit skills. The Independent Challenges increase in difficulty, with the first one in each unit being the easiest. Independent Challenges 2 and 3 become increasingly open-ended, requiring more independent problem solving.
- **Advanced Challenge Exercises** set within the Independent Challenges provide optional steps for more advanced students.
- **Visual Workshops** are practical, self-graded capstone projects that require independent problem solving.

Instructor Resources

The Instructor Resources CD is Course Technology's way of putting the resources and information needed to teach and learn effectively into your hands. With an integrated array of teaching and learning tools that offer you and your students a broad range of technology-based instructional options, we believe this CD represents the highest quality and most cutting edge resources available to instructors today. Many of these resources are available at *www.course.com*. The resources available with this book are:

- **Instructor's Manual**—Available as an electronic file, the Instructor's Manual includes detailed lecture topics with teaching tips for each unit.
- **Sample Syllabus**—Prepare and customize your course easily using this sample course outline.
- **PowerPoint Presentations**—Each unit has a corresponding PowerPoint presentation that you can use in lecture, distribute to your students, or customize to suit your course.
- **Figure Files**—The figures in the text are provided on the Instructor Resources CD to help you illustrate key topics or concepts. You can create traditional overhead transparencies by printing the figure files. Or you can create electronic slide shows by using the figures in a presentation program such as PowerPoint.
- **Data Files for Students**—To complete most of the units in this book, your students will need Data Files. You can post the Data Files on a file server for students to copy. The Data Files are available on the Instructor Resource CD-ROM, the Review Pack, and can also be downloaded from www.course.com.

Instruct students to use the Data Files List included on the Review Pack and the Instructor Resource CD. This list gives instructions on copying and organizing files.

- **Solutions to Exercises**—Solutions to Exercises contains every file students are asked to create or modify in the lessons and end-of-unit material. Also provided in this section, there is a document outlining the solutions for the end-of-unit Concepts Review, Skills Review, and Independent Challenges. An Annotated Solution File and Grading Rubric accompany each file and can be used together for quick and easy grading.
- **ExamView**—ExamView is a powerful testing software package that allows you to create and administer printed, computer (LAN-based), and Internet exams. ExamView includes hundreds of questions that correspond to the topics covered in this text, enabling students to generate detailed study guides that include page references for further review. The computer-based and Internet testing components allow students to take exams at their computers, and also saves you time by grading each exam automatically.

CourseCasts—Learning on the Go. Always Available…Always Relevant.

Want to keep up with the latest technology trends relevant to you? Visit our site to find a library of podcasts, CourseCasts, featuring a "CourseCast of the Week," and download them to your mp3 player at *http://coursecasts.course.com*.

Our fast-paced world is driven by technology. You know because you're an active participant—always on the go, always keeping up with technological trends, and always learning new ways to embrace technology to power your life.

Ken Baldauf, a faculty member of the Florida State University Computer Science Department, is responsible for teaching technology classes to thousands of FSU students each year. He knows what you know; he knows what you want to learn. He's also an expert in the latest technology and will sort through and aggregate the most pertinent news and information so you can spend your time enjoying technology, rather than trying to figure it out.

Visit us at *http://coursecasts.course.com* to learn on the go!

Assessment & Training Solutions

SAM 2007

SAM 2007 helps bridge the gap between the classroom and the real world by allowing students to train and test on important computer skills in an active, hands-on environment.

SAM 2007's easy-to-use system includes powerful interactive exams, training, or projects on critical applications such as Word, Excel, Access, PowerPoint, Outlook, Windows, the Internet, and much more. SAM simulates the application environment, allowing students to demonstrate their knowledge and think through the skills by performing real-world tasks.

Designed to be used with the Illustrated series, SAM 2007 includes built-in page references so students can print helpful study guides that match the Illustrated textbooks used in class. Powerful administrative options allow instructors to schedule exams and assignments, secure tests, and run reports with almost limitless flexibility.

Student Edition Labs

Our Web-based interactive labs help students master hundreds of computer concepts, including input and output devices, file management and desktop applications, computer ethics, virus protection, and much more. Featuring up-to-the-minute content, eye-popping graphics, and rich animation, the highly interactive Student Edition Labs offer students an alternative way to learn through dynamic observation, step-by-step practice, and challenging review questions. Also available on CD at an additional cost.

Online Content   Blackboard

Blackboard is the leading distance learning solution provider and class-management platform today. Course Technology has partnered with Blackboard to bring you premium online content. Instructors: Content for use with this text is available in a Blackboard Course Cartridge and may include topic reviews, case projects, review questions, test banks, practice tests, custom syllabi, and more.

Course Technology also has solutions for several other learning management systems. Please visit *www.course.com* today to see what's available for this title.

Read This Before You Begin

Frequently Asked Questions

What software was used to write and test this book?

This book was written and tested using a typical installation of Microsoft Office 2007 installed on a computer with a typical installation of Microsoft Windows Vista with Aero turned off. For more information on turning Aero on and off or restoring other default settings, see the Appendix at the end of this book.

The browser used for any steps that require a browser is Internet Explorer 7.

Do I need to be connected to the Internet to complete the steps and exercises in this book?

Some of the exercises in this book assume that your computer is connected to the Internet. If you are not connected to the Internet, see your instructor for information on how to complete the exercises.

What do I do if my screen is different from the figures shown in this book?

This book was written and tested on computers with monitors set at a resolution of 1024 × 768. If your screen shows more or less information than the figures in the book, your monitor is probably set at a higher or lower resolution. If you don't see something on your screen, you might have to scroll down or up to see the object identified in the figures.

The Ribbon (the blue area at the top of the screen) in Microsoft Office 2007 adapts to different resolutions. If your monitor is set at a lower resolution than 1024 × 768, you might not see all of the buttons shown in the figures. The groups of buttons will always appear, but the entire group might be condensed into a single button that you need to click to access the buttons described in the instructions. For example, the figures and steps in this book assume that the Editing group on the Home tab in Word looks like the following:

1024 × 768 Editing Group

Editing Group on the Home Tab of the Ribbon at 1024 × 768

If your resolution is set to 800 × 600, the Ribbon in Word will look like the following figure, and you will need to click the Editing button to access the buttons that are visible in the Editing group.

800 × 600 Editing Group

Editing Group on the Home Tab of the Ribbon at 800 × 600

800 × 600 Editing Group Clicked

Editing Group on the Home Tab of the Ribbon at 800 × 600 is selected to show available buttons

Getting Started with Microsoft Office 2007

Files You Will Need:

OFFICE A-1.xlsx

Microsoft Office 2007 is a group of software programs designed to help you create documents, collaborate with co-workers, and track and analyze information. Each program is designed so you can work quickly and efficiently to create professional-looking results. You use different Office programs to accomplish specific tasks, such as writing a letter or producing a sales presentation, yet all the programs have a similar look and feel. Once you become familiar with one program, you'll find it easy to transfer your knowledge to the others. ▓▓▓ This unit introduces you to the most frequently used programs in Office, as well as common features they all share.

OBJECTIVES

Understand the Office 2007 Suite

Start and exit an Office program

View the Office 2007 user interface

Create and save a file

Open a file and save it with a
   new name

View and print your work

Get Help and close a file

Understanding the Office 2007 Suite

Microsoft Office 2007 features an intuitive, context-sensitive user interface, so you can get up to speed faster and use advanced features with greater ease. The programs in Office are bundled together in a group called a **suite** (although you can also purchase them separately). The Office suite is available in several configurations, but all include Word and Excel. Other configurations include PowerPoint, Access, Outlook, Publisher, and/or others. Each program in Office is best suited for completing specific types of tasks, though there is some overlap in terms of their capabilities.

The Office programs covered in this book include:

- **Microsoft Office Word 2007**

  When you need to create any kind of text-based document, such as memos, newsletters, or multi-page reports, Word is the program to use. You can easily make your documents look great by inserting eye-catching graphics and using formatting tools such as themes. **Themes** are predesigned combinations of color and formatting attributes you can apply, and are available in most Office programs. The Word document shown in Figure A-1 was formatted with the Solstice theme.

- **Microsoft Office Excel 2007**

  Excel is the perfect solution when you need to work with numeric values and make calculations. It puts the power of formulas, functions, charts, and other analytical tools into the hands of every user, so you can analyze sales projections, figure out loan payments, and present your findings in style. The Excel worksheet shown in Figure A-1 tracks personal expenses. Because Excel automatically recalculates results whenever a value changes, the information is always up-to-date. A chart illustrates how the monthly expenses are broken down.

- **Microsoft Office PowerPoint 2007**

  Using PowerPoint, it's easy to create powerful presentations complete with graphics, transitions, and even a soundtrack. Using professionally designed themes and clip art, you can quickly and easily create dynamic slideshows such as the one shown in Figure A-1.

- **Microsoft Office Access 2007**

  Access helps you keep track of large amounts of quantitative data, such as product inventories or employee records. The form shown in Figure A-1 was created for a grocery store inventory database. Employees use the form to enter data about each item. Using Access enables employees to quickly find specific information such as price and quantity, without hunting through store shelves and stockrooms.

Microsoft Office has benefits beyond the power of each program, including:

- **Common user interface: Improving business processes**

  Because the Office suite programs have a similar **interface**, or look and feel, your experience using one program's tools makes it easy to learn those in the other programs. Office documents are **compatible** with one another, meaning that you can easily incorporate, or **integrate**, an Excel chart into a PowerPoint slide, or an Access table into a Word document.

- **Collaboration: Simplifying how people work together**

  Office recognizes the way people do business today, and supports the emphasis on communication and knowledge-sharing within companies and across the globe. All Office programs include the capability to incorporate feedback—called **online collaboration**—across the Internet or a company network.

FIGURE A-1: Microsoft Office 2007 documents

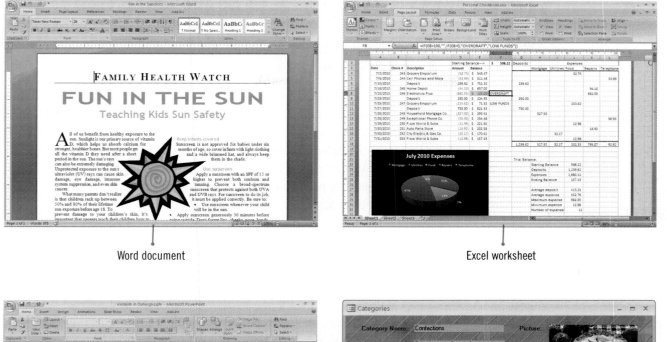

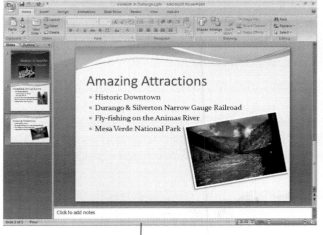

Word document

Excel worksheet

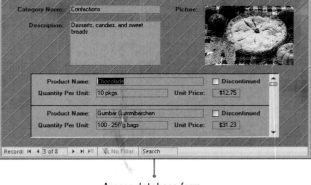

PowerPoint presentation

Access database form

Deciding which program to use

Every Office program includes tools that go far beyond what you might expect. For example, although Excel is primarily designed for making calculations, you can use it to create a database. So when you're planning a project, how do you decide which Office program to use? The general rule of thumb is to use the program best suited for your intended task, and make use of supporting tools in the program if you need them. Word is best for creating text-based documents, Excel is best for making mathematical calculations, PowerPoint is best for preparing presentations, and Access is best for managing quantitative data. Although the capabilities of Office are so vast that you *could* create an inventory in Excel or a budget in Word, you'll find greater flexibility and efficiency by using the program designed for the task. And remember, you can always create a file in one program, and then insert it in a document in another program when you need to, such as including sales projections (Excel) in a memo (Word).

Starting and Exiting an Office Program

The first step in using an Office program is of course to open, or **launch**, it on your computer. You have a few choices for how to launch a program, but the easiest way is to click the Start button on the Windows taskbar, or to double-click an icon on your desktop. You can have multiple programs open on your computer simultaneously, and you can move between open programs by clicking the desired program or document button on the taskbar or by using the [Alt][Tab] keyboard shortcut combination. ▓▓▓ When working, you'll often want to open multiple programs in Office, and switch among them throughout the day. Begin by launching a few Office programs now.

STEPS

QUICK TIP

You can also launch a program by double-clicking a desktop icon or clicking an entry on the Recent Items menu.

1. **Click the Start button ⊕ on the taskbar**

   The Start menu opens, as shown in Figure A-2. If the taskbar is hidden, you can display it by pointing to the bottom of the screen. Depending on your taskbar property settings, the taskbar may be displayed at all times, or only when you point to that area of the screen. For more information, or to change your taskbar properties, consult your instructor or technical support person.

2. **Point to All Programs, click Microsoft Office, then click Microsoft Office Word 2007**

   Microsoft Office Word 2007 starts and the program window opens on your screen.

QUICK TIP

It is not necessary to close one program before opening another.

3. **Click ⊕ on the taskbar, point to All Programs, click Microsoft Office, then click Microsoft Office Excel 2007**

   Microsoft Office Excel 2007 starts and the program window opens, as shown in Figure A-3. Word is no longer visible, but it remains open. The taskbar displays a button for each open program and document. Because this Excel document is **active**, or in front and available, the Microsoft Excel – Book1 button on the taskbar appears in a darker shade.

4. **Click Document1 – Microsoft Word on the taskbar**

   Clicking a button on the taskbar activates that program and document. The Word program window is now in front, and the Document1 – Microsoft Word taskbar button appears shaded.

QUICK TIP

If there isn't room on your taskbar to display the entire name of each button, you can point to any button to see the full name in a Screentip.

5. **Click ⊕ on the taskbar, point to All Programs, click Microsoft Office, then click Microsoft Office PowerPoint 2007**

   Microsoft Office PowerPoint 2007 starts, and becomes the active program.

6. **Click Microsoft Excel – Book1 on the taskbar**

   Excel is now the active program.

QUICK TIP

As you work in Windows, your computer adapts to your activities. You may notice that after clicking the Start button, the name of the program you want to open appears in the Start menu; if so, you can click it to start the program.

7. **Click ⊕ on the taskbar, point to All Programs, click Microsoft Office, then click Microsoft Office Access 2007**

   Microsoft Office Access 2007 starts, and becomes the active program.

8. **Point to the taskbar to display it, if necessary**

   Four Office programs are open simultaneously.

9. **Click the Office button ⊕, then click Exit Access, as shown in Figure A-4**

   Access closes, leaving Excel active and Word and PowerPoint open.

FIGURE A-2: **Start menu**

FIGURE A-3: **Excel program window and Windows taskbar**

Excel button
on taskbar

Word button
on taskbar

Your icons in the notification
area will differ

FIGURE A-4: **Exiting Microsoft Office Access**

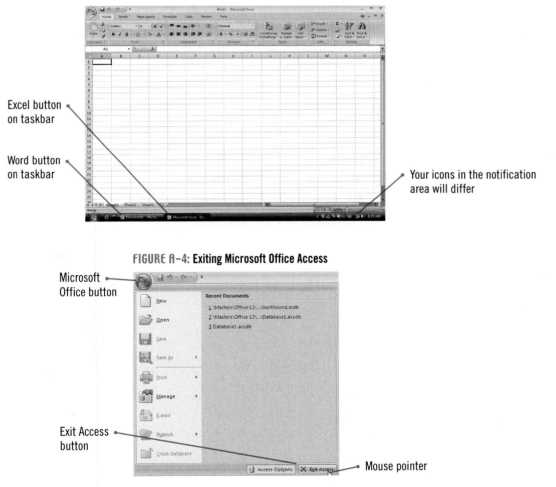

Microsoft
Office button

Exit Access
button

Mouse pointer

Using shortcut keys to move between Office programs

As an alternative to the Windows taskbar, you can use a keyboard shortcut to move among open Office programs. The [Alt][Tab] keyboard combination lets you either switch quickly to the next open program, or choose one from a palette. To switch immediately to the next open program, press [Alt][Tab]. To choose from all open programs, press and hold [Alt], then press and release [Tab] without releasing [Alt]. A palette opens on screen, displaying the icon and filename of each open program and file. Each time you press [Tab] while holding [Alt], the selection cycles to the next open file. Release [Alt] when the program/file you want to activate is selected.

Viewing the Office 2007 User Interface

One of the benefits of using Office is that the programs have much in common, making them easy to learn and making it simple to move from one to another. Individual Office programs have always shared many features, but the innovations in the Office 2007 user interface mean even greater similarity among them all. That means you can also use your knowledge of one program to get up to speed in another. A **user interface** is a collective term for all the ways you interact with a software program. The user interface in Office 2007 includes a more intuitive way of choosing commands, working with files, and navigating in the program window. ▰▰▰ Familiarize yourself with some of the common interface elements in Office by examining the PowerPoint program window.

STEPS

1. **Click** Microsoft PowerPoint – [Presentation1] **on the taskbar**

   PowerPoint becomes the active program. Refer to Figure A-5 to identify common elements of the Office user interface. The **document window** occupies most of the screen. In PowerPoint, a blank slide appears in the document window, so you can build your slide show. At the top of every Office program window is a **title bar**, which displays the document and program name. Below the title bar is the **Ribbon**, which displays commands you're likely to need for the current task. Commands are organized into **tabs**. The tab names appear at the top of the Ribbon, and the active tab appears in front with its name highlighted. The Ribbon in every Office program includes tabs specific to the program, but all include a Home tab on the far left, for the most popular tasks in that program.

2. **Click the** Office button ⊙

   The Office menu opens. This menu contains commands common to most Office programs, such as opening a file, saving a file, and closing the current program. Next to the Office button is the **Quick Access toolbar**, which includes buttons for common Office commands.

3. **Click** ⊙ **again to close it, then point to the** Save button 🖫 **on the Quick Access toolbar, but do not click it**

   You can point to any button in Office to see a description; this is a good way to learn the available choices.

4. **Click the** Design tab **on the Ribbon**

   To display a different tab, you click its name on the Ribbon. Each tab arranges related commands into **groups** to make features easy to find. The Themes group displays available themes in a **gallery**, or palette of choices you can browse. Many groups contain a **dialog box launcher**, an icon you can click to open a dialog box or task pane for the current group, which offers an alternative way to choose commands.

5. **Move the mouse pointer** ⌖ **over the** Aspect theme **in the Themes group as shown in Figure A-6,** *but do not click the mouse button*

   Because you have not clicked the theme, you have not actually made any changes to the slide. With the **Live Preview** feature, you can point to a choice, see the results right in the document, and then decide whether you want to make the change.

6. **Move** ⌖ **away from the Ribbon and towards the slide**

   If you clicked the Aspect theme, it would be applied to this slide. Instead, the slide remains unchanged.

7. **Point to the** Zoom slider 🔱 **on the status bar, then drag** 🔱 **to the right until the Zoom percentage reads** 166%

   The slide display is enlarged. Zoom tools are located on the status bar. You can drag the slider or click the plus and minus buttons to zoom in/out on an area of interest. The percentage tells you the zoom effect.

8. **Drag the** Zoom slider 🔱 **on the status bar to the left until the Zoom percentage reads** 73%

FIGURE A-5: PowerPoint program window

Quick Access toolbar
Ribbon
Dialog box launcher
Zoom percentage
Title bar
Tabs
Document window
Zoom slider

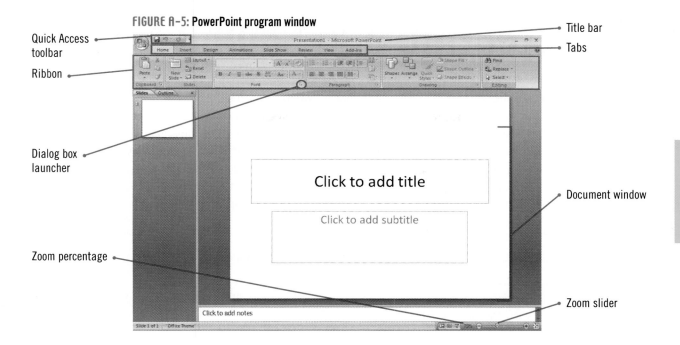

FIGURE A-6: Viewing a theme with Live Preview

Aspect theme
Mouse pointer
ScreenTip
Current zoom percentage
Zoom slider

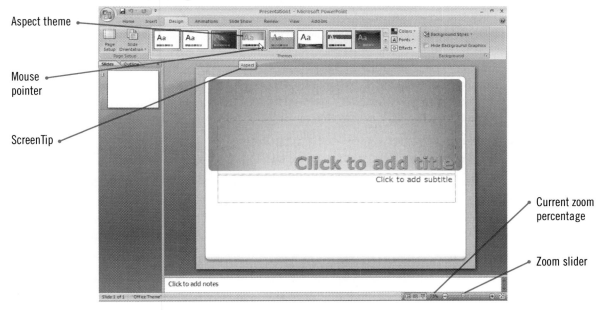

Office 2007

Customizing the Quick Access toolbar

You can customize the Quick Access toolbar to display your favorite commands. To do so, click the Customize Quick Access Toolbar button ⏷ in the title bar, then click the command you want to add. If you don't see the command in the list, click More Commands to open the Customize tab of the Options dialog box. In the Options dialog box, use the Choose commands from list to choose a category, click the desired command in the list on the left, click Add to add it to the Quick Access toolbar, then click OK. To remove a button from the toolbar, click the name in the list on the right, then click Remove. To add a command to the Quick Access toolbar on the fly, simply right-click the button on the Ribbon, then click Add to Quick Access Toolbar on the shortcut menu. You can also use the Customize Quick Access Toolbar button to move the toolbar below the ribbon, by clicking Show Below the Ribbon, or to minimize the Ribbon so it takes up less space onscreen. If you click Minimize the Ribbon, the Ribbon is minimized to display only the tabs. When you click a tab, the Ribbon opens so you can choose a command; once you choose a command, the Ribbon closes again, and only the tabs are visible.

Creating and Saving a File

When working in a program, one of the first things you need to do is to create and save a file. A **file** is a stored collection of data. Saving a file enables you to work on a project now, then put it away and work on it again later. In some Office programs, including Word, Excel, and PowerPoint, a new file is automatically created when you start the program, so all you have to do is enter some data and save it. In Access, you must expressly create a file before you enter any data. You should give your files meaningful names and save them in an appropriate location, so they're easy to find. ▰▰▰▰ Use Microsoft Word to familiarize yourself with the process of creating and saving a document. First you'll type some notes about a possible location for a corporate meeting, then you'll save the information for later use.

STEPS

1. **Click Document1 – Microsoft Word on the taskbar**

2. **Type Locations for Corporate Meeting, then press [Enter] twice**
   The text appears in the document window, and a cursor blinks on a new blank line. The cursor indicates where the next typed text will appear.

3. **Type Las Vegas, NV, press [Enter], type Orlando, FL, press [Enter], type Chicago, IL, press [Enter] twice, then type your name**
   Compare your document to Figure A-7.

QUICK TIP

A filename can be up to 255 characters, including a file extension, and can include upper- or lowercase characters and spaces, but not ?, ", /, \, <, >, *, |, or :.

4. **Click the Save button 🖫 on the Quick Access toolbar**
   Because this is the first time you are saving this document, the Save As dialog box opens, as shown in Figure A-8. The Save As dialog box includes options for assigning a filename and storage location. Once you save a file for the first time, clicking 🖫 saves any changes to the file *without* opening the Save As dialog box, because no additional information is needed. In the Address bar, Office displays the default location for where to save the file, but you can change to any location. In the File name field, Office displays a suggested name for the document based on text in the file, but you can enter a different name.

QUICK TIP

You can create a desktop icon that you can double-click to both launch a program and open a document, by saving it to the desktop.

5. **Type Potential Corporate Meeting Locations**
   The text you type replaces the highlighted text.

6. **In the Save As dialog box, use the Address bar or Navigation pane to navigate to the drive and folder where you store your Data Files**
   Many students store files on a flash drive or Zip drive, but you can also store files on your computer, a network drive, or any storage device indicated by your instructor or technical support person.

QUICK TIP

To create a new blank file when a file is open, click the Office button, click New, then click Create.

7. **Click Save**
   The Save As dialog box closes, the new file is saved to the location you specified, then the name of the document appears in the title bar, as shown in Figure A-9. (You may or may not see a file extension.) See Table A-1 for a description of the different types of files you create in Office, and the file extensions associated with each. You can save a file in an earlier version of a program by choosing from the list of choices in the Save as type list arrow in the Save As dialog box.

TABLE A-1: Common filenames and default file extensions

File created in	is called a	and has the default extension
Excel	workbook	.xlsx
Word	document	.docx
Access	database	.accdb
PowerPoint	presentation	.pptx

FIGURE A-7: Creating a document in Word

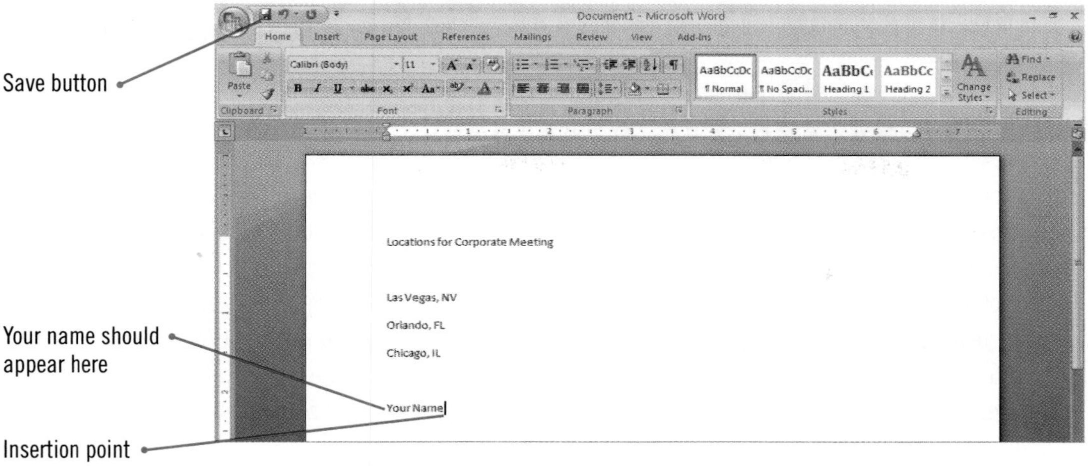

Save button
Your name should appear here
Insertion point
Document1 - Microsoft Word
Locations for Corporate Meeting
Las Vegas, NV
Orlando, FL
Chicago, IL
Your Name

FIGURE A-8: Save As dialog box

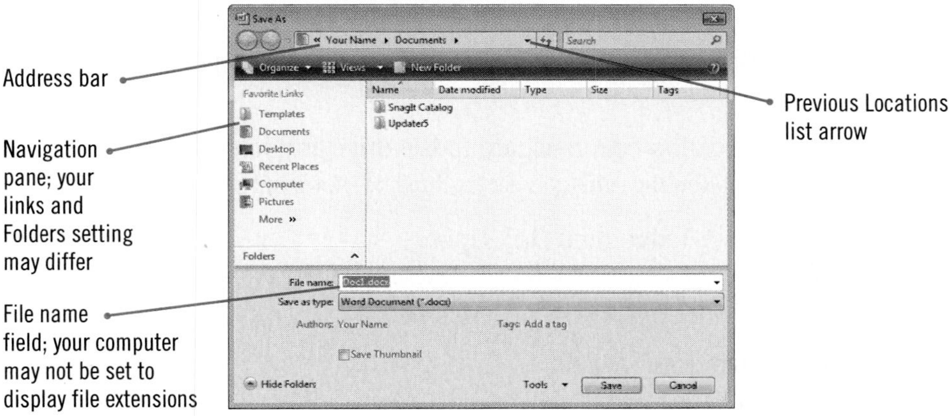

Address bar
Navigation pane; your links and Folders setting may differ
File name field; your computer may not be set to display file extensions
Previous Locations list arrow
Save As
File name:
Save as type: Word Document (*.docx)
Save
Cancel

FIGURE A-9: Named Word document

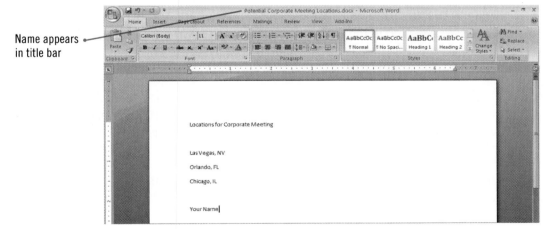

Name appears in title bar
Potential Corporate Meeting Locations.docx - Microsoft Word
Locations for Corporate Meeting
Las Vegas, NV
Orlando, FL
Chicago, IL
Your Name

Using the Office Clipboard

You can use the Office Clipboard to cut and copy items from one Office program and paste them into others. The Clipboard can store a maximum of 24 items. To access it, open the Office Clipboard task pane by clicking the launcher in the Clipboard group in the Home tab. Each time you copy a selection, it is saved in the Office Clipboard. Each entry in the Office Clipboard includes an icon that tells you the program in which it was created. To paste an entry, click in the document where you want it to appear, then click the item in the Office Clipboard. To delete an item from the Office Clipboard, right-click the item, then click Delete.

Opening a File and Saving it with a New Name

In many cases as you work in Office, you start with a blank document, but often you need to use an existing file. It might be a file you or a co-worker created earlier as a work-in-progress, or it could be a complete document that you want to use as the basis for another. For example, you might want to create a budget for this year using the budget you created last year; you could type in all the categories and information from scratch, or you could open last year's budget, save it with a new name, and just make changes to update it for the current year. By opening the existing file and saving it with the Save As command, you create a duplicate that you can modify to your heart's content, while the original file remains intact. Use Excel to open an existing workbook file, and save it with a new name so the original remains unchanged.

STEPS

QUICK TIP

If you point to a command on the Office menu that is followed by an arrow, a submenu opens displaying additional, related commands.

1. **Click Microsoft Excel – Book1 on the taskbar, click the Office button 🔘, then click Open**

   The Open dialog box opens, where you can navigate to any drive or folder location accessible to your computer to locate a file.

2. **In the Open dialog box, navigate to the drive and folder where you store your Data Files**

   The files available in the current folder are listed, as shown in Figure A-10. This folder contains one file.

3. **Click OFFICE A-1.xlsx, then click Open**

   The dialog box closes and the file opens in Excel. An Excel file is an electronic spreadsheet, so it looks different from a Word document or a PowerPoint slide.

QUICK TIP

The Recent Items list on the Office menu displays recently opened documents; you can click any file to open it.

4. **Click 🔘, then click Save As**

   The Save As dialog box opens, and the current filename is highlighted in the File name text box. Using the Save As command enables you to create a copy of the current, existing file with a new name. This action preserves the original file, and creates a new file that you can modify.

5. **Navigate to the drive and folder where your Data Files are stored if necessary, type Budget for Corporate Meeting in the File name text box, as shown in Figure A-11, then click Save**

   A copy of the existing document is created with the new name. The original file, Office A-1.xlsx, closes automatically.

QUICK TIP

The Save As command works identically in all Office programs, except Access; in Access, this command lets you save a copy of the current database object, such as a table or form, with a new name, but not a copy of the entire database.

6. **Click cell A19, type your name, then press [Enter], as shown in Figure A-12**

   In Excel, you enter data in cells, which are formed by the intersection of a row and a column. Cell A19 is at the intersection of column A and row 19. When you press [Enter], the cell pointer moves to cell A20.

7. **Click the Save button 🔲 on the Quick Access toolbar**

   Your name appears in the worksheet, and your changes to the file are saved.

Exploring File Open options

You might have noticed that the Open button on the Open dialog box includes an arrow. In a dialog box, if a button includes an arrow you can click the button to invoke the command, or you can click the arrow to choose from a list of related commands. The Open button list arrow includes several related commands, including Open Read-Only and Open as Copy. Clicking Open Read-Only opens a file that you can only save by saving it with a new name; you cannot save changes to the original file. Clicking Open as Copy creates a copy of the file already saved and named with the word "Copy" in the title. Like the Save As command, these commands provide additional ways to use copies of existing files while ensuring that original files do not get inadvertently changed.

FIGURE A-10: Open dialog box

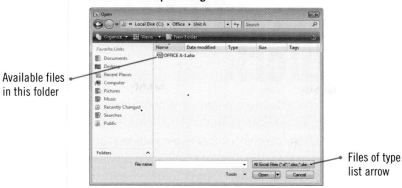

Available files
in this folder

Files of type
list arrow

FIGURE A-11: Save As dialog box

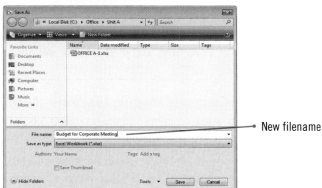

New filename

FIGURE A-12: Adding your name to the worksheet

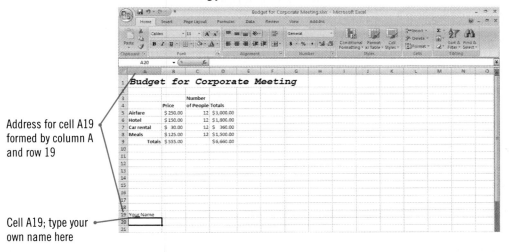

Address for cell A19
formed by column A
and row 19

Cell A19; type your
own name here

Working in Compatibility mode

Not everyone upgrades to the newest version of Office. As a general rule, new software versions are **backward-compatible**, meaning that documents saved by an older version can be read by newer software. The reverse is not always true, so Office 2007 includes a feature called Compatibility mode. When you open a file created in an earlier version of Office, "Compatibility Mode" appears in the title bar, letting you know the file was created in an earlier, but usable version of the program. If you are working with someone who may not be using the newest version of the software, you can avoid possible incompatibility problems by saving your file in another, earlier format. To do this, click the Office button, point to the Save As command, then click a choice on the Save As submenu. For example, if you're working in Excel, click Excel 97-2003 Workbook format. When the Save As dialog box opens, you'll notice that the Save as type box reads "Excel 97-2003 Workbook" instead of the default "Excel Workbook." To see more file format choices, such as Excel 97-2003 Template or Microsoft Excel 5.0/95 Workbook, click Other Formats on the Save As submenu. In the Save As dialog box, click the Save as type button, click the choice you think matches what your co-worker is using, then click Save.

Viewing and Printing Your Work

If your computer is connected to a printer or a print server, you can easily print any Office document. Printing can be as simple as clicking a button, or as involved as customizing the print job by printing only selected pages or making other choices, and/or **previewing** the document to see exactly what a document will look like when it is printed. (In order for printing and previewing to work, a printer must be installed.) In addition to using Print Preview, each Microsoft Office program lets you switch among various **views** of the document window, to show more or fewer details or a different combination of elements that make it easier to complete certain tasks, such as formatting or reading text. You can also increase or decrease your view of a document, so you can see more or less of it on the screen at once. Changing your view of a document does not affect the file in any way, it affects only the way it looks on screen. Experiment with changing your view of a Word document, and then preview and print your work.

STEPS

1. **Click Potential Corporate Meeting Locations – Microsoft Word on the taskbar**
   Word becomes the active program, and the document fills the screen.

2. **Click the View tab on the Ribbon**
   In most Office programs, the View tab on the Ribbon includes groups and commands for changing your view of the current document. You can also change views using the View buttons on the status bar.

3. **Click Web Layout button in the Document Views group on the View tab**
   The view changes to Web Layout view, as shown in Figure A-13. This view shows how the document will look if you save it as a Web page.

   > **QUICK TIP**
   > You can also use the Zoom button in the Zoom group of the View tab to enlarge or reduce a document's appearance.

4. **Click the Zoom in button ⊕ on the status bar eight times until the zoom percentage reads 180%**
   Zooming in, or choosing a higher percentage, makes a document appear bigger on screen, but less of it fits on the screen at once; **zooming out**, or choosing a lower percentage, lets you see more of the document but at a reduced size.

5. **Drag the Zoom slider ▽ on the status bar to the center mark**
   The Zoom slider lets you zoom in and out without opening a dialog box or clicking buttons.

6. **Click the Print Layout button on the View tab**
   You return to Print Layout view, the default view in Microsoft Word.

7. **Click the Office button ⊛, point to Print, then click Print Preview**
   The Print Preview presents the most accurate view of how your document will look when printed, displaying the entire page on screen at once. Compare your screen to Figure A-14. The Ribbon in Print Preview contains a single tab, also known as a **program** tab, with commands specific to Print Preview. The commands on this tab facilitate viewing and changing overall settings such as margins and page size.

   > **QUICK TIP**
   > You can open the Print dialog box from any view by clicking the Office button, then clicking Print.

8. **Click the Print button on the Ribbon**
   The Print dialog box opens, as shown in Figure A-15. You can use this dialog box to change which pages to print, the number of printed copies, and even the number of pages you print on each page. If you have multiple printers from which to choose, you can change from one installed printer by clicking the Name list arrow, then clicking the name of the installed printer you want to use.

9. **Click OK, then click the Close Print Preview button on the Ribbon**
   A copy of the document prints, and Print Preview closes.

FIGURE A-13: Web Layout view

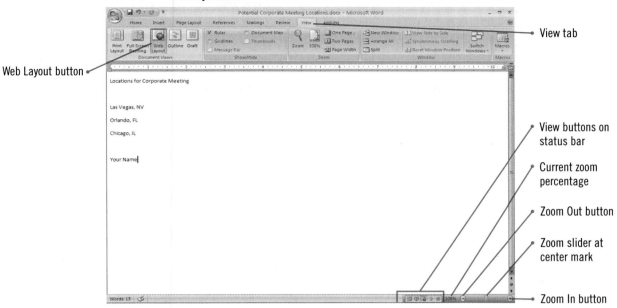

Web Layout button

View tab

View buttons on status bar

Current zoom percentage

Zoom Out button

Zoom slider at center mark

Zoom In button

FIGURE A-14: Print Preview screen

Print button

Orientation button

Zoom button

Close Print Preview button

FIGURE A-15: Print dialog box

Your selected printer will be different

Print range options let you choose which pages to print

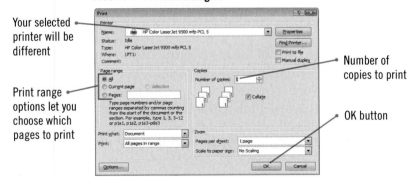

Number of copies to print

OK button

Using the Print Screen feature to create a screen capture

At some point you may want to create a screen capture. A **screen capture** is a snapshot of your screen, as if you took a picture of it with a camera. You might want to take a screen capture if an error message occurs and you want Technical Support to see exactly what's on the screen. Or perhaps your instructor wants to see what your screen looks like when you create a particular document. To create a screen capture, press [PrtScn]. (Keyboards differ, but you may

find the [PrtScn] button on the Insert key in or near your keyboard's function keys. You may have to press the [F Lock] key to enable the Function keys.) Pressing this key places a digital image of your screen in the Windows temporary storage area known as the **Clipboard**. Open the document where you want the screen capture to appear, click the Home tab on the Ribbon (if necessary), then click Paste on the Home tab. The screen capture is pasted into the document.

Getting Help and Closing a File

You can get comprehensive help at any time by pressing [F1] in an Office program. You can also get help in the form of a ScreenTip by pointing to almost any icon in the program window. When you're finished working in an Office document, you have a few choices regarding ending your work session. You can close a file or exit a program by using the Office button or by clicking a button on the title bar. Closing a file leaves a program running, while exiting a program closes all the open files in that program as well as the program itself. In all cases, Office reminds you if you try to close a file or exit a program and your document contains unsaved changes. ▰▰▰▰▰ Explore the Help system in Microsoft Office, and then close your documents and exit any open programs.

STEPS

1. **Point to the Zoom button on the View tab of the Ribbon**

   A ScreenTip appears that describes how the Zoom button works.

QUICK TIP

If you are not connected to the Internet, the Help window displays only the help content available on your computer.

2. **Press [F1]**

   The Word Help window opens, as shown in Figure A-16, displaying the home page for help in Word. Each entry is a hyperlink you can click to open a list of related topics. This window also includes a toolbar of useful Help commands and a Search field. The connection status at the bottom of the Help window indicates that the connection to Office Online is active. Office Online supplements the help content available on your computer with a wide variety of up-to-date topics, templates, and training.

3. **Click the Getting help link in the Table of Contents pane**

   The icon next to Getting help changes and its list of subtopics expands.

QUICK TIP

You can also open the Help window by clicking the Microsoft Office Help button 🔘 to the right of the tabs on the Ribbon.

4. **Click the Work with the Help window link in the topics list in the left pane**

   The topic opens in the right pane, as shown in Figure A-17.

5. **Click the Hide Table of Contents button 🔲 on the Help toolbar**

   The left pane closes, as shown in Figure A-18.

QUICK TIP

You can print the current topic by clicking the Print button 🖨 on the Help toolbar to open the Print dialog box.

6. **Click the Show Table of Contents button 📖 on the Help toolbar, scroll to the bottom of the left pane, click the Accessibility link in the Table of Contents pane, click the Use the keyboard to work with Ribbon programs link, read the information in the right pane, then click the Help window Close button**

7. **Click the Office button 🔘, then click Close; if a dialog box opens asking whether you want to save your changes, click Yes**

   The Potential Corporate Meeting Locations document closes, leaving the Word program open.

8. **Click 🔘, then click Exit Word**

   Microsoft Office Word closes, and the Excel program window is active.

9. **Click 🔘, click Exit Excel, click the PowerPoint button on the taskbar if necessary, click 🔘, then click Exit PowerPoint**

   Microsoft Office Excel and Microsoft Office PowerPoint both close.

FIGURE A-16: Word Help window

Help toolbar

Search field

Hide Table of
Contents
button

The colors
of your links
may differ

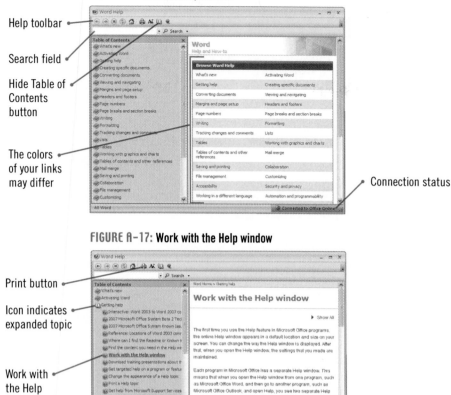

Connection status

FIGURE A-17: Work with the Help window

Print button

Icon indicates
expanded topic

Work with
the Help
window link

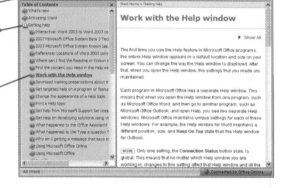

FIGURE A-18: Help window with Table of Contents closed

Show Table of
Contents button

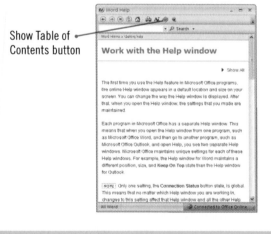

Recovering a document

Sometimes while you are using Office, you may experience a power failure or your computer may "freeze," making it impossible to continue working. If this type of interruption occurs, each Office program has a built-in recovery feature that allows you to open and save files that were open at the time of the interruption. When you restart the program(s) after an interruption, the Document Recovery task pane opens on the left side of your screen displaying both original and recovered versions of the files that were open. If you're not sure which file to open (original or recovered), it's usually better to open the recovered file because it will contain the latest information. You can, however, open and review all versions of the file that were recovered and save the best one. Each file listed in the Document Recovery task pane displays a list arrow with options that allow you to open the file, save it as is, delete it, or show repairs made to it during recovery.

Practice

▼ CONCEPTS REVIEW

Label the elements of the program window shown in Figure A-19.

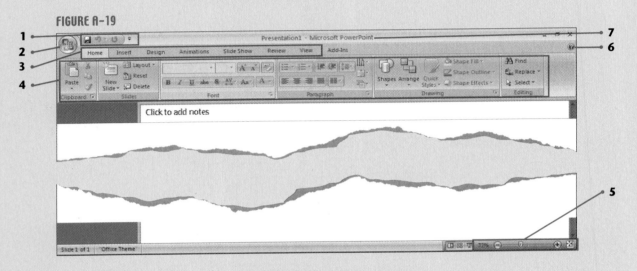

FIGURE A-19

Match each project with the program for which it is best suited.

8. Microsoft Office PowerPoint
9. Microsoft Office Excel
10. Microsoft Office Word
11. Microsoft Office Access

a. Corporate expansion budget with expense projections
b. Business résumé for a job application
c. Auto parts store inventory
d. Presentation for Board of Directors meeting

▼ INDEPENDENT CHALLENGE 1

You just accepted an administrative position with a local car dealership that's recently invested in computers and is now considering purchasing Microsoft Office. You are asked to propose ways Office might help the dealership. You produce your proposal in Microsoft Word.

a. Start Word, then save the document as **Microsoft Office Proposal** in the drive and folder where you store your Data Files.

b. Type **Microsoft Office Word**, press [Enter] twice, type **Microsoft Office Excel**, press [Enter] twice, type **Microsoft Office PowerPoint**, press [Enter] twice, type **Microsoft Office Access**, press [Enter] twice, then type your name.

c. Click the line beneath each program name, type at least two tasks suited to that program, then press [Enter].

d. Save your work, then print one copy of this document.

Advanced Challenge Exercise

■ Press the [PrtScn] button to create a screen capture, then press [Ctrl][V].

■ Save and print the document.

e. Exit Word.

Getting Started with E-Mail

E-mail is an essential communication tool for business and personal correspondence. You can use a desktop information management program like Microsoft Office Outlook 2007, or any of several Web-based e-mail programs, to send and receive e-mail. Once you learn the basic features of e-mail, you will be able to use Outlook or any other e-mail program to manage your e-mail.  You are an assistant to Juan Ramirez, the personnel director at Quest Specialty Travel (QST). Much of the correspondence in the company is through e-mail. Juan wants you to learn the basics of e-mail for your job.

OBJECTIVES

Communicate with e-mail

Compile an e-mail address book

Create and send a message

Manage e-mail folders

Receive and reply to a message

Forward a message

Send a message with an attachment

Employ good e-mail practices

Communicating with E-Mail

Electronic mail (e-mail) is the technology that makes it possible for you to send and receive messages through the Internet. The messages sent using e-mail technology are known as **e-mail messages**, or **e-mail** for short. **E-mail software** enables you to send and receive e-mail messages over a network, over an intranet, and over the Internet. A **computer network** is the hardware and software that makes it possible for two or more computers to share information and resources. An **intranet** is a computer network that connects computers in a local area only, such as computers in a company's office. The **Internet** is a network of connected computers and computer networks located around the world. Figure A-1 illustrates how e-mail messages can travel over a network. Quest Specialty Travel employees use e-mail to communicate with each other and with clients because it is fast, reliable, and easy.

DETAILS

E-mail enables you to:

QUICK TIP

E-mail uses store-and-forward technology: Messages are *stored* on a service provider's computer until a recipient logs on to a computer and requests his or her messages. At that time, the messages are *forwarded* to the recipient's computer.

- **Communicate conveniently and efficiently**

  E-mail is an effective way to correspond with coworkers or colleagues. E-mail can be sent from one person to another person or a group of people anywhere in the world. You can send and receive messages directly from any computer with an Internet or network connection. E-mail can also be sent and received from wireless devices such as cell phones and PDAs with e-mail capability. Unlike the postal service, e-mail is delivered almost instantaneously. Recipients do not have to be at their computers at the same time that a message is sent in order to receive the message.

- **Send images and sound as well as text information**

  Messages can be formatted so that they are easy to read and appear professional and attractive. Messages can include graphics in the body of the message to convey visual information. In addition, you can attach files, such as a sound or video, photographs, graphics, spreadsheets, or word-processing documents, to a message.

- **Communicate with several people at once**

  You can create your own electronic address book that stores the names and e-mail addresses of people with whom you frequently communicate. You can then send the same message to more than one person at one time.

- **Ensure the delivery of information**

  With e-mail software such as Outlook, you have the option of receiving a delivery confirmation message when a recipient receives your e-mail. In addition, if you are away and unable to access e-mail because of a vacation or other plans, you can set up an automatic message that is delivered to senders so they are alerted to the fact that you might not receive your e-mail for a specified time period.

- **Correspond from a remote place**

  If you have an Internet connection and communications software, you can connect to your computer from a remote location, and you can send and receive messages from any location. You can sign up with an ISP (Internet service provider) to send and receive e-mail. If you are using Web-based e-mail, you can access your e-mail from any computer that is connected to the Internet from anywhere in the world. You can connect to the Internet using a telephone line or use other, faster technologies including satellite, DSL (Digital Subscriber Line), cable, fiber optic, ISDN (Integrated Services Digital Network), T1, or T3.

- **Organize a record of your communications**

  You can organize the messages you send and receive in a way that best suits your working style. You can store e-mail messages in folders and refer to them again in the future. Organizing your saved messages lets you keep a record of communications, which can be very valuable in managing a project or business. You can also flag messages to give an instant visual cue that distinguishes those messages that require immediate attention from those that can wait. Depending on the service provider, you can download e-mail to your computer or keep it on the provider's Web server. If e-mail is stored on the Web, you can access it from any computer anywhere in the world that has Internet access.

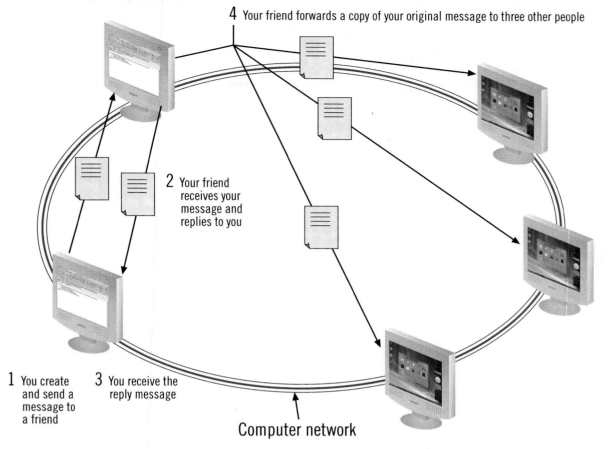

4 Your friend forwards a copy of your original message to three other people

2 Your friend receives your message and replies to you

1 You create and send a message to a friend

3 You receive the reply message

Computer network

The medium is the message

When you communicate with e-mail, take extra care in what you say and how you say it. The recipient of an e-mail message doesn't have the benefit of seeing body language or hearing the tone of voice to interpret the meaning of the message. For example, using all capital letters in the text of a message is the e-mail equivalent of shouting and is not appropriate. Carefully consider the content of a message before you send it, and don't send confidential or sensitive material. Remember, once you send a message, you might not be able to prevent it from being delivered. E-mail is not private; you cannot control who might read the message once it has been sent. Do not write anything in an e-mail that you would not write on a postcard that you send through the postal service. If your e-mail account is a company account, be sure you know the policy on whether or not your company permits the sending of personal messages. All messages you send through an employer's e-mail system have been legally interpreted as property of the company for which you work, so don't assume that your messages are private.

Compiling an E-Mail Address Book

E-mail can be sent from one person to another person or a group of people anywhere in the world. To send and receive e-mail over the Internet using an e-mail program, you must have an e-mail address. Each person has his or her own e-mail address and a password that lets him or her log in to an e-mail program and receive e-mail. To send an e-mail message, you need to know the e-mail address of the person to whom you are sending the message. A person can have more than one e-mail address. At Quest Specialty Travel, each employee is assigned an e-mail address. As the assistant to the personnel director in the Human Resources department, you maintain a list of all employee e-mail addresses in an electronic address book that you use to distribute information about company policies and events through e-mail. You review the parts of an e-mail address and the benefits of maintaining an e-mail address book.

DETAILS

An e-mail address has three parts:

- **Username**

  The first part of an e-mail address is the username. The username identifies the person who receives the e-mail sent to the e-mail address. At Quest Specialty Travel, as in many companies, universities, or organizations, usernames are assigned and are based on a specified format. At QST, a username is the first initial of the person's first name and the last name. In many e-mail systems, such as those used primarily for personal e-mail, you get to create your username, combining letters and numbers to create a unique username for your e-mail address.

- **@ sign**

  The middle part of an e-mail address is the @ sign, called an "at sign." It separates the username from the service provider or e-mail provider name. Every e-mail address includes an @ sign.

- **Service provider or e-mail provider**

  The last part of the e-mail address is the service provider or e-mail provider. There are many different service providers. For example, the service provider might be the name of the company a person works for or the name of the school where the person goes to school. The service provider generally is a company or organization that provides the connection to the Internet and provides e-mail. The service provider can also be the Web site name for Web-based e-mail. Table A-1 provides some examples of e-mail address formats that are used with different service providers.

The benefits of an e-mail address book include the following:

- **Stores the names and e-mail addresses of people to whom you frequently send e-mail messages**

  Instead of having to remember the address of someone to whom you are sending an e-mail, you can select the name you want from a stored list of names and e-mail addresses. Outlook 2007 and several other e-mail programs refer to the address book entries as "contacts" and place them in a folder called Contacts. When you create a new contact, you enter the person's full name and e-mail address. You may also have the option to enter additional information about that person, including his or her personal and business mailing address, telephone number, cell phone number, Web page, Instant Message address, and even a picture.

- **Reduces errors and makes using e-mail quicker and more convenient**

  Being able to select a contact from your address book saves you from having to type someone's e-mail address each time you want to send a message. It also reduces the chance that your message will not be delivered because you typed the e-mail address incorrectly. In most e-mail programs, if someone sends you a message, you can click the address in the message header to add it directly to your address book without any errors. Figure A-2 shows a sample address book from Outlook 2007.

FIGURE A-2: Address Book

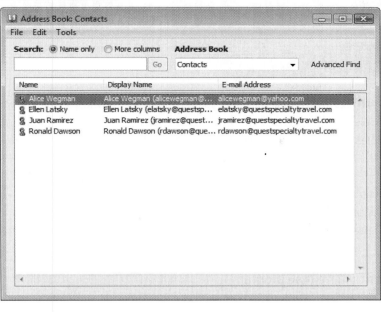

TABLE A-1: E-mail providers and formats for e-mail addresses

e-mail sponsor	example service provider	description of e-mail services	where e-mail is stored	sample e-mail addresses
Corporate or company e-mail	Quest Specialty Travel	A travel company that provides e-mail for employees	Company server, but also can be downloaded to user's computer	username@questspecialtytravel.com
Internet Service Provider: Cable television, voice and data communications company	America Online Comcast Cablevision Earthlink Verizon	Commercial Internet service providers provide Internet access as well as other Internet services, including Web space and several e-mail addresses for subscribers for a monthly fee	ISP server, until user accesses e-mail; then it is downloaded to user's computer	username@aol.com username@comcast.net username@optonline.net username@earthlink.net username@verizon.net
Web based e-mail	Hotmail—Microsoft's Web-based e-mail service Gmail—Google's Web-based e-mail service Yahoo! Mail—Yahoo!'s Web-based e-mail service	Web site that provides free e-mail addresses and service for individuals who sign up	On the Web site e-mail server	username@hotmail.com username@gmail.com username@yahoo.com
Educational institution	Harvard University	Colleges and universities provide e-mail for faculty, staff, and students	On the university e-mail server	username@harvard.edu

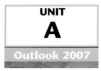

Creating and Sending a Message

When you create an e-mail message, you must indicate to whom you are sending the message and specify any people who should receive a copy. You also need to enter a meaningful subject for the message to give its recipients an idea of its content. You write the text of your message in the **message body**. After you create the message, you send it. Outlook 2007 uses Microsoft Word as the default text editor in e-mail messages, which means that you have access to the same text-formatting features in Outlook that you use when you create Word documents. Most e-mail programs use a basic text editor that enables you to do such things as change the color of text, use different fonts, create a bulleted list, and check the spelling of your message. ▬▬▬ You write and send a message to several employees about an upcoming meeting.

STEPS

> **QUICK TIP**
> Make sure you know your username and password so that you can log in to your e-mail program.

1. **Start your e-mail program**

   If you are using Outlook 2007 or another e-mail program, you start the application and then create a message without connecting to the Internet. If your e-mail program is Web-based, such as Hotmail or Gmail, you have to be connected to the Internet to create an e-mail message. You go to the Web site that sponsors your e-mail, and log in to your account.

2. **Click the button or link that allows you to create new mail, such as the New Mail Message button or the Compose Mail button**

   All e-mail programs provide a button or link to use to begin writing a new message. There are basic similarities in all programs, in that each new message window or page provides boxes or spaces to enter address information and message content, as shown in Figure A-3.

> **QUICK TIP**
> Use the e-mail address of a friend or associate to complete this lesson, or use your own e-mail address.

3. **Enter a valid e-mail address in the To text box as the address of the person to whom you are sending the message**

   You can send e-mail to more than one person at one time; just type each e-mail address in the To text box, and separate the addresses with a semi-colon or comma (depending on what your e-mail program requires). Click the To button or the Address Book button to open the address book and select each e-mail address from the address book. If you click names or e-mail addresses in an address book, you are less likely to make an error as you enter addresses. You can send e-mail to recipients even if they are not already in your address book by typing each e-mail address directly in the To text box.

> **QUICK TIP**
> Message headers include the names and e-mail addresses of recipients and CC recipients, but not of BCC recipients.

4. **Click the Cc text box, then type a friend's e-mail address as the e-mail address for a recipient who is to receive a courtesy copy**

   CC stands for courtesy copy. **Courtesy copies** are typically sent to message recipients who need to be aware of the correspondence between the sender and the recipients. BCC, or **blind courtesy copy**, is used when the sender does not want to reveal who he or she has sent courtesy copies to. You can use the address book to enter addresses into the Cc and Bcc text boxes.

5. **Type Meeting July 10 in the Subject box as the subject for your message**

   The Subject text box should be a brief statement that indicates the purpose of your message. The subject becomes the title of the message.

> **QUICK TIP**
> Although you can write and read messages in Outlook and other programs when you are not online, you must be connected to the Internet to send or receive messages.

6. **Type your message in the message window**

   Figure A-4 shows a sample completed message. Many e-mail programs provide a spell-checking program that enables you to make sure that you do not have spelling errors in your message. Messages should be concise and polite. If you want to send a lengthy message, you can consider attaching a file to the message. (You will learn about attaching files later in this unit.)

7. **Click the Send button to send your e-mail message**

   Once the message is sent, the message window or Web page closes. Most e-mail programs store a copy of the message in your Sent or Sent Items folder, or give you the option to do so.

FIGURE A-3: New message window

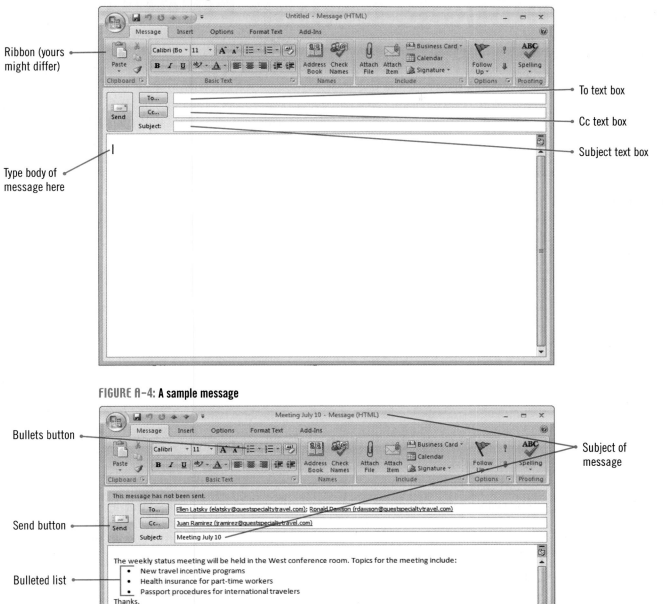

Ribbon (yours might differ)

To text box

Cc text box

Subject text box

Type body of message here

FIGURE A-4: A sample message

Bullets button

Subject of message

Send button

Bulleted list

Body text

This message has not been sent.

To... Ellen Latsky (elatsky@questspecialtytravel.com); Ronald Dawson (rdawson@questspecialtytravel.com)

Cc... Juan Ramirez (jramirez@questspecialtytravel.com)

Subject: Meeting July 10

The weekly status meeting will be held in the West conference room. Topics for the meeting include:
- New travel incentive programs
- Health insurance for part-time workers
- Passport procedures for international travelers
Thanks.

Message headers

A message header contains the basic information about a message. When e-mail travels through the e-mail system, the message header is the first information that you see when you retrieve your e-mail. Message headers include the sender's name and e-mail address, the names and e-mail addresses of recipients and CC recipients, a date and time stamp, and the subject of the message. E-mail programs date-stamp e-mail messages when they are received at the recipient's computer.

Manage E-Mail Folders

Just as files are saved in folders on your computer, e-mail messages can be saved in folders within an e-mail program. Although there are many different e-mail programs, they all provide a way for you to organize and save e-mail messages. You save messages so that you can refer to them again in the future when needed. Most e-mail programs come with several default folders. These include Inbox, Sent Items, Outbox, Deleted Items, and Junk E-mail folders (or folders with similar names). See Figure A-5. In addition, most allow you to create additional personalized folders with meaningful names. Once you save messages, you can sort the messages within the folders to help you find the message you want. ▰▰▰▰ As an employee of the Human Resources department, you send and receive messages on several topics. You organize the e-mail so you can better track the messages you send and receive.

DETAILS

E-mail programs come with the following default folders:

- **Inbox**

    An Inbox is a mail folder that stores all incoming e-mail. All e-mail arrives in the Inbox as it is received. You know who sent the e-mail message because the username or e-mail address and subject line appear in the list of e-mail in your Inbox, as shown in Figure A-6. You will also know when the message came in because your computer puts a date on it, which you can see along with the username and subject line. A closed envelope icon means the message has not been read yet. Many e-mail systems allow you to preview the message header before opening a message. You can organize e-mail by date, sender, subject, and other header data.

QUICK TIP
You should clear out the Sent Items and Deleted Items folders periodically to free up storage space on your computer.

- **Sent Items**

    When you send a message, a copy of the message is stored in the Sent Items folder. The Sent Items folder helps you track the messages that you send out. You can change the settings on most e-mail programs so that you do not have to save messages to the Sent Items folder. You may not want to save all sent messages because they take up storage space on your computer.

- **Outbox**

    The Outbox is a temporary storage folder for messages that have not yet been sent. If you are working offline or if you set your e-mail program so that messages do not get sent immediately after you click the Send button, the messages are placed in the Outbox. When you connect to the Internet or click the Send/Receive button, the messages in the Outbox are sent.

- **Deleted Items or Trash**

    When you delete or erase a message from any folder, it is placed in the Deleted Items or Trash folder rather than being immediately and permanently deleted. This means that if you delete a message accidentally, you can find it again. To empty the Deleted Items folder, you have to right-click the folder or click a menu or toolbar button, and then click Empty Deleted Items Folder. Some programs have a special link to click in order to empty the folder. Some Web-based e-mail programs clear out the Trash folder if it gets too full or after messages have been in the folder for a specified period of time.

- **Junk E-mail or Spam**

    Junk e-mail, or spam, is unwanted e-mail that arrives from unsolicited sources. Most junk e-mail is advertising or offensive messages. **Spamming** is the sending of identical or near-identical unsolicited messages to a large number of recipients. Many e-mail programs have filters that identify this type of e-mail and place it in a special folder. This gives you the option of easily deleting the e-mail you don't want. It is possible that a message that you do want may get caught by the spam filter. It is good practice to look at the headers in the Junk E-mail folder before deleting the messages stored there.

FIGURE A-5: Mail Folders

FIGURE A-6: Message headers in Inbox

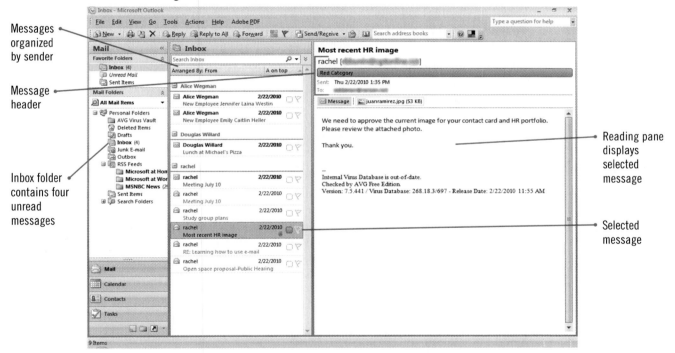

Messages organized by sender

Message header

Inbox folder contains four unread messages

Reading pane displays selected message

Selected message

Sorting the mail

You would be surprised at how quickly your Inbox, Sent Items, and Deleted Items or Trash folders can fill up. How can you manage these? The best way is to create folders for specific projects or people that you know will be "high-volume" for e-mail. For example, if you are working on a special project, create a folder for that project. Any e-mail that you receive or send about the project can be moved into that folder. You can sort e-mail by any message header, such as date,

subject, or sender, to find an important message quickly. Once the project is completed, you can archive or delete that folder's e-mail. You should also be mindful as to how much e-mail is accumulating in the Deleted Items or Trash folder. E-mail takes up storage space and if you are running out of storage on your computer, your e-mail is a good place to start cleaning up the hard drive.

Receiving and Replying to a Message

To read a message that arrives in your Inbox, you first select it. Outlook and some other e-mail software programs let you preview each message when it is selected in the Reading or Preview Pane. To open the message in its own window, you can double-click the message header, or right-click the message header, then click Open from the shortcut menu. After reading a message, you can delete it, move it to another folder, flag it for follow-up, or keep it in your Inbox. You can also send a response back to the sender of the message by clicking the Reply button. Or, you can reply simultaneously to the sender of an e-mail message and everyone to whom the original message was sent by clicking the Reply to All button. A reply is a common e-mail activity. You often reply to messages sent to you as you correspond with the staff at QST.

1. **Open a new message window, enter** your e-mail address **in the To text box, type** Learning how to use e-mail **as the subject, then for the body of the message, type** I am sending this message to myself to learn how to send and reply to messages.

TROUBLE
You may have to check for mail several times before the e-mail message comes in.

2. **Click the** Send button **in the message window, click the** Send/Receive button **or click the** Get Mail **or** Check Mail button **or link, then open the** Inbox **in the e-mail program**
   When you click the Send/Receive or Get Mail button, your e-mail program checks for any messages in the Outbox that need to be sent and delivers incoming messages to your Inbox. Many e-mail programs deliver e-mail to the Inbox at the time you sign in or log in with your username and password.

3. **Click the** Learning how to use e-mail message **in the Inbox to select it, if necessary**
   You can read the message header to identify the message by subject, date, and sender. If your e-mail has a preview feature, you can preview the message before you open it. In Outlook, the message is shown in the Reading Pane. A preview generally permits you to view the first few lines of a message; you might have to click a link or button to display images. Many programs hide images to protect your privacy, unless you configure the program's settings to accept images for each message in the Inbox.

QUICK TIP
In Web-based e-mail programs, clicking an e-mail message opens the message. Skip Step 4 if this is the case.

4. **Double-click the** message, **click the** message **once, or click** Open
   You can view the entire message in a new window or Web page, as shown in Figure A-7. When you view a message, you will see buttons for several options available to you after you read the message. One of the options is a Reply button or link. You generally have two options for replying. One is to reply to the original sender. The other is a Reply to All option. When you click Reply to All, you reply to the original sender and all the CC recipients of the original message. BCC recipients are not included in Reply or Reply to All messages.

5. **Click the** Reply button
   A new message window for replying opens. Clicking the Reply button automatically addresses the e-mail to the original sender. The subject line is preceded by "RE:", indicating that the message is a reply. The message header from the original message appears in the message window above the original message. The insertion point is at the top of the message body. See Figure A-8.

QUICK TIP
Depending on your program preferences, your reply font color might be a color other than black.

6. **Type** I am learning how to use many e-mail features. **in the message body as the reply**
   It is helpful to include the original message in a reply so that the recipient of the message can be reminded of the topic. Depending on how you set up your e-mail program, you can automatically include or exclude the text of the original sender's message in the message body along with the message header.

7. **Click the** Send button **in the message window**
   The message is sent and a copy of it is stored in your Sent Items folder. Most e-mail programs will add a Replied to Message icon next to the original message in the Inbox indicating that you have replied to the message.

8. **Close the original message if necessary to return to the Inbox**

FIGURE A-7: Message opened

Click to reply to original sender only

Click to reply to original sender and all Cc recipients

The addresses on your screen will be different

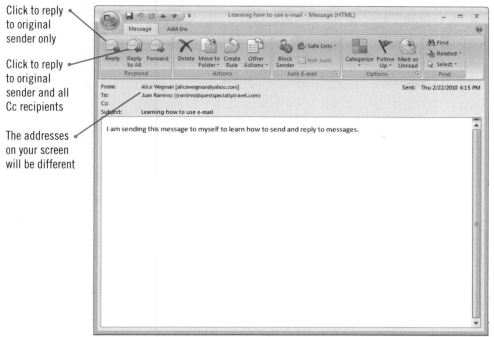

FIGURE A-8: Replying to a message

Address of original sender automatically entered in To box for reply

Indicates a reply e-mail

Insertion point is here for reply text in message

Original message

The addresses on your screen will be different

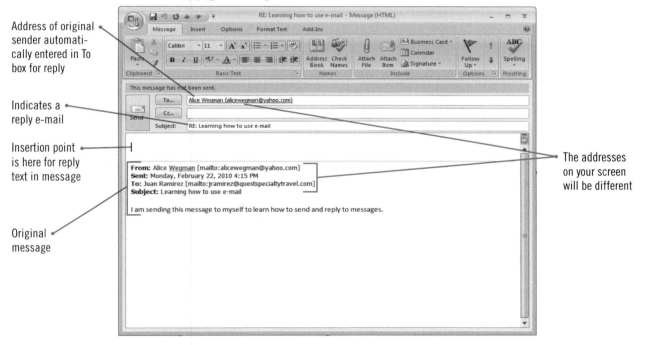

Vacation responses

Most e-mail programs allow you to set up an automatic response or vacation message if you are not going to be able to get your e-mail for a specified period of time. This is a helpful way to let people know that you are not ignoring any e-mail they send, but rather that you are not reading your e-mail. When vacation mode is active, your e-mail program automatically sends out a reply when a message comes in. You determine the parameters and content of the reply message. A typical message might be "Thank you for your message. I am on vacation from July 1–July 10th and will respond to your message when I return." Most e-mail programs only send one Auto Response to each sender each day or within a specified period of time.

Forwarding a Message

You may receive e-mail that you need to send to someone else. Sending a message you have received from one person to someone else is called **forwarding**. When you forward a message, you send it to people who have not already received it – that is, people not in the To or Cc text boxes of the original message. You can include an additional message about the forwarded message in the message body. The subject of the forwarded message stays the same, so it can be organized by subject with any other messages in a string of messages on the same topic and with the same subject heading. In most e-mail programs, you forward a message that you have received to another person by clicking the Forward button. At QST, you sometimes get e-mail from clients that you forward to the travel agents at their branch offices for their information.

STEPS

1. **Click the Send/Receive button or click the Get Mail or Check Mail button or link in the e-mail program**

   Your e-mail program checks for any messages in the Outbox that need to be sent and delivers messages to your Inbox.

   QUICK TIP
   Skip Step 3 if clicking the message opens the message rather than selects it.

2. **Click any message in the Inbox that you want to forward to select it, if necessary**

   You read the message header to identify the message. You can see the original recipients of the message by reviewing the header. You can see who, if anyone, got the message by reviewing the e-mail addresses in the To and Cc areas of the header. You will not know who might have received a BCC on the message. You determine if this message needs to be forwarded to anyone.

3. **Double-click the message, click the message once, or click Open to open the message**

   You view the entire message in a new window or Web page. When you view a message, you see buttons for several options available to you after you read the message. One of the options is to use the Forward button to forward the message.

4. **Click the Forward button**

   A new Message window opens containing the original message. Clicking the Forward button does not automatically address the e-mail to anyone; all address fields are blank. The original message is included in the body of the message. The subject line is preceded by "FW:", indicating that the message is a forwarded one. Most e-mail software includes the message header from the original message in the Message window above the original message. The insertion point is at the top of the message window in the To field. You can address this message as you would any new e-mail. You can include multiple recipients, including CC and BCC recipients. If you want to provide a courtesy note explaining the forward, you can click in the message body above the original message header and type a brief note.

5. **Type a friend's e-mail address in the To text box, then type I thought you might like to read this message. in the message body above the forwarded message, as shown in Figure A-9**

6. **Click the Send button in the message window**

   The message is sent, and a copy of it is stored in your Sent Items folder. Most e-mail programs add a Forwarded Message icon next to the original message indicating that you have forwarded the message. Often this is a small arrow pointing to the right.

7. **Close the original message if necessary to return to the Inbox**

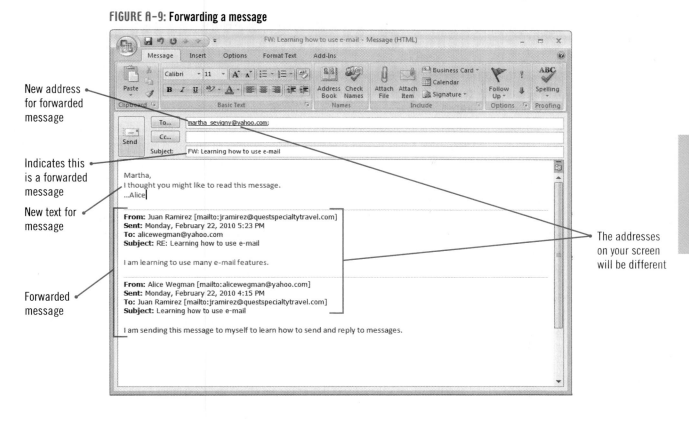

New address for forwarded message

Indicates this is a forwarded message

New text for message

Forwarded message

The addresses on your screen will be different

Flagging or labeling messages

Most e-mail programs provide a way to identify or categorize e-mail. If you use e-mail for business, school, or personal communication, you will find that you receive many e-mail messages. Some can be read and discarded. Others require additional attention or follow-up. Organizing your e-mail can help you keep up with the many messages you are likely to receive. If you are using Outlook, flags can assist you in your effort to manage your e-mail. If you click the flag icon next to the message, it is marked by default with a red Quick Flag. However, you can use flags of different shades of red to mark messages for different categories of follow-up. In Outlook, flags are available for Today, Tomorrow, This Week, Next Week, No Date and Custom; the Today flag is the darkest shade of red, and the This Week and Next Week flags are the lightest. To apply a flag, select the message you want to flag, click Actions on the menu bar, point to Follow Up, then click the flag you want to use to categorize the message. You can also right-click the message, then point to Follow Up to apply a flag. To select from a list of flag actions and specify a due date in the Custom dialog box, right-click a message, point to Follow Up, then click Add Reminder. If you are using Web-based e-mail, you may have other options for labeling or flagging e-mail.

For example, Gmail provides a way to assign a label to e-mail or to star e-mail for easy sorting or organizing. See Figure A-10.

FIGURE A-10: Flagging messages

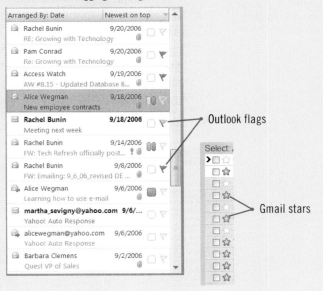

Outlook flags

Gmail stars

Sending a Message with an Attachment

In addition to composing a message by typing in the Message window to send an e-mail message to someone, you can **attach** a file to an e-mail message. For example, in an office environment, employees can attach Word or Excel documents to e-mail messages so that other employees can open them, make changes to them, and then return them to the original sender or forward them to others for review. You can attach any type of computer file to an e-mail message, including pictures, video clips, and audio clips. Keep in mind that to open an attachment created using a particular software program, the recipient of the attachment must have the appropriate software. You often send clients' trip photos to people in the office. You also have to send personnel documents to employees throughout the year. Attaching files is a common task in your job in the Human Resources department.

STEPS

1. **In your e-mail program, click the button or link to open a new mail message window, then type your e-mail address in the To text box**

   You can send a message with an attachment to more than one person at one time; just enter each e-mail address in the To text box, separated by a semi-colon or comma, just as you would an e-mail without an attachment. You can also click the Cc text box or Bcc text box, and then enter e-mail addresses for recipients who are to receive a CC or BCC.

2. **Type New Logo in the Subject box as the subject for the message, then type Here is the new logo for you to review. as the message in the message window**

3. **Click the Insert File, Attach File, or Attach button**

   Most e-mail programs provide a way to attach files, but the name of the command or way to access the dialog box may differ slightly. Once the Attach File or Insert File dialog box opens, files appear in a dialog box as shown in Figure A-11. You may have to click a Browse button to navigate to the file or files you want to attach. Often you can use Thumbnails view in the dialog box to see what the files look like before you attach them to a message.

   TROUBLE

   Attachments such as movies may be too large for some e-mail systems to handle.

4. **Navigate to the drive and folder where you store your Data Files, click QST Logo.jpg, then click Insert, Open, or Attach**

   Most programs will allow you to attach more than one file to a message. Some Internet service providers will limit message size or the number of attachments for one e-mail. Once attached, files appear in the Attach text box or other area of the message window. Often, an icon next to each filename indicates the type of file it is. The numbers in parentheses next to the filenames specify the size of each file. As a rule of thumb, try to keep the total size of attachments below 1 MB. Also, consider the Internet connection speed of the recipient's computer. If a recipient does not have a fast Internet connection, a large file could take a long time to download.

5. **Send the message**

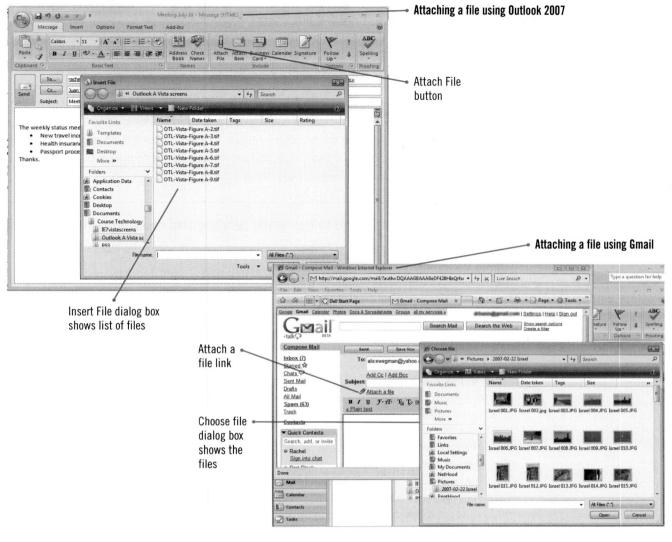

Attaching a file using Outlook 2007

Attach File button

Insert File dialog box shows list of files

Attaching a file using Gmail

Attach a file link

Choose file dialog box shows the files

Options when sending messages

E-mail programs can have several options that affect how messages are delivered. To change these options in Outlook, click the launcher 🔲 in the Options group on the Message tab in the Message window to open the Message Options dialog box shown in Figure A-12. You can, for example, assign a level of importance and a level of sensitivity so that the reader can prioritize messages. You can also encrypt the message for privacy. If both the sender and recipient are using Outlook, you can add Voting buttons to your message for recipients to use in responding. In addition, when you want to know when a message has been received or read, you can select the Request a delivery receipt for this message check box or the Request a read receipt for this message check box. You can also specify a future date for delivering a message, if the timing of the message is important. Lastly, if you want replies to your message to be sent to a different e-mail address than your own, you can click the Have replies sent to check box and then specify a new destination address for replies.

FIGURE A-12: Outlook 2007 Message Options dialog box

Employing Good E-Mail Practices

E-mail has become the standard for business correspondence. It has also become an accepted standard for personal communication as well as communication between students and teachers. Although it is an easy and fast way to communicate, there are many considerations to keep in mind before sending e-mail. 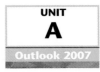 Working in the Human Resources department, you are responsible for corporate policy relating to e-mail. You send out a note that outlines the company policy for e-mail.

DETAILS

The following are good practices to follow when sending and receiving e-mail:

- Always be polite and use proper spelling and grammar in e-mail messages. Be sure to use the spelling checker as a last step before sending messages.
- Unless you have consulted with the recipient and know that they can receive large file attachments, avoid sending any attachment that exceeds 1MB. Consider using compression software to reduce the size of any attachment that exceeds the limit but must be sent.
- Never open an e-mail message unless you know who sent it to you. Keep your spam filter, spyware software, and virus software up-to-date. Be sure to run the virus checker through all received e-mail. Keeping computers safe from viruses and spyware is very important.
- Before you forward a message, consider the contents of the message and the privacy of the person who sent the message. A joke, a story, or anything that is not personal usually can be forwarded without invading the sender's privacy. When you are certain the sender would not mind having his or her message forwarded, you can forward the message to others.
- In very casual correspondence, you can present an informal message by using shortcuts like "LOL" for "laughing out loud" and "BRB!" for "be right back!" However, limit this technique to personal messages. Any e-mail that is intended for professional use or is a reflection on a professional organization should not use shortcuts. See Figure A-13.
- You can use emoticons in your text to show how you are feeling. You create an emoticon by combining more than one keyboard character to make a graphic. The use of emoticons should also be limited to informal e-mail among close colleagues or friends, not professional correspondence. Examples of some popular emoticons are shown in Table A-2.
- When you are finished using an e-mail program, it is good practice to delete e-mail messages that you no longer need. You should delete files periodically from the Sent folder to help manage storage on your computer. It is also good practice to empty the Trash folder. To delete a file, you select a file, then click the Delete button or press the Delete key. To empty the Trash or Deleted Items folder, you right-click the folder, then click Empty Trash or Empty Deleted Items folder. See Figure A-14.

Distribution lists

When using an e-mail program to communicate with friends or coworkers, you may find that you need to send messages to the same group of people on a regular basis. If your address book contains many contacts, it can take time to scroll through all the names to select the ones you want, and you might forget to include someone in an important message. Fortunately, e-mail programs provide an easy way to group your contacts. You can create a **distribution list**, or a **group**, which is a collection of contacts to whom you want to send the same messages. Distribution lists make it possible for you to send a message to the same group without having to select each contact in the group. For example, if you send messages reminding your Human Resources staff of a weekly meeting, you can create a distribution list called "HR-STAFF" that contains the names and e-mail addresses of your staff who must attend the meeting. When you want to send a message to everyone on the team, you simply select HR-STAFF from the address book, instead of selecting each person's name individually. Once a distribution list is created, you can add new members to it, or delete members from it, as necessary. If you change information about a contact that is part of a distribution list, the distribution list is automatically updated.

FIGURE A-13: E-mail shortcuts

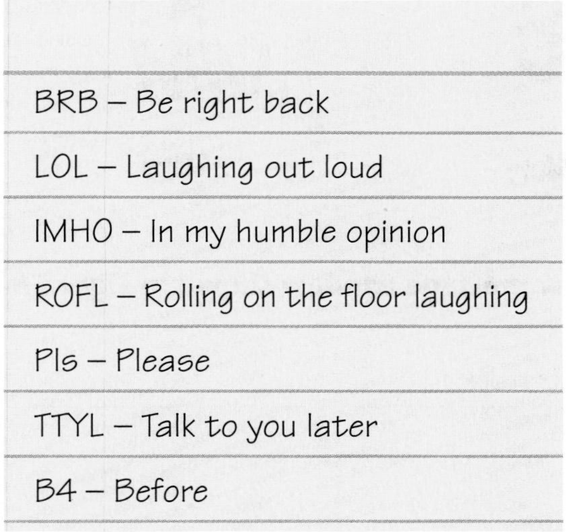

BRB – Be right back
LOL – Laughing out loud
IMHO – In my humble opinion
ROFL – Rolling on the floor laughing
Pls – Please
TTYL – Talk to you later
B4 – Before

FIGURE A-14: Confirm before permanently deleting all the items

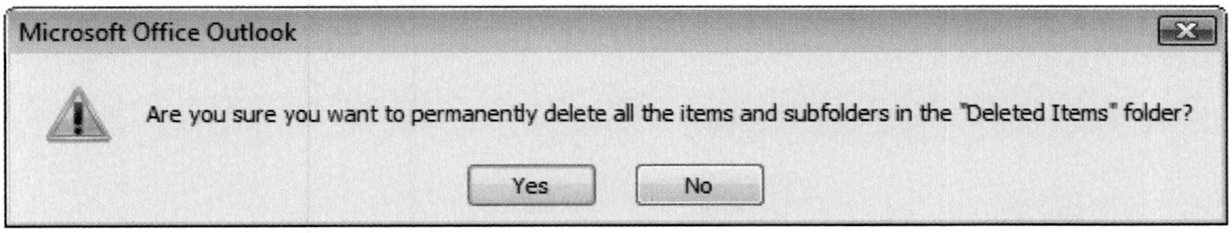

Microsoft Office Outlook

Are you sure you want to permanently delete all the items and subfolders in the "Deleted Items" folder?

Yes   No

TABLE A-2: Popular emoticons

keys	result	emoticon name	
colon and closed parenthesis	:)	smiley	
semicolon and closed parenthesis	;)	wink	
colon and open parenthesis	:(	sad	
colon, dash, capital D	:-D	person laughing	
equal sign, dash, o	=-o	surprised	
colon, dash, slash	:-\	undecided	
8, dash, closed parenthesis	8-)	cool	

Practice

▼ CONCEPTS REVIEW

Label the elements of the new message window shown in Figure A-15.

FIGURE A-15: New message window

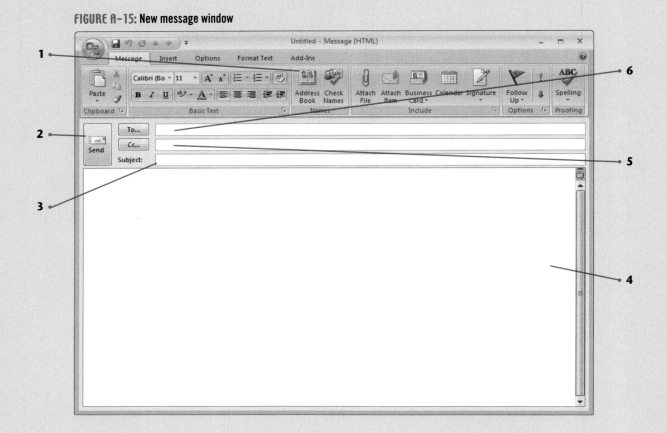

Match each term with the statement that best describes it.

7. **E-mail**
8. **Attachment**
9. **Bcc**
10. **Sent Items folder**
11. **Inbox**
12. **Address book**

a. Stores names and e-mail addresses
b. Stores all e-mail that you send out
c. A computer file that is sent along with an e-mail message
d. Message that is sent and received over a computer network
e. Contains messages you have received
f. Hides e-mail address of recipient to all others

Select the best answer from the list of choices.

13. Any e-mail received as part of large unsolicited mailing is best placed in the _____.
- **a.** Junk E-Mail or Spam folder
- **b.** Deleted Items folder
- **c.** Sent Items folder
- **d.** Inbox

14. Which of the following statements is true about sending file attachments?
- **a.** You can only send one attachment with each e-mail message.
- **b.** Only recipients listed in the To text box will get the attachment.
- **c.** There is no limit on the size or number of attachments you can send with a message.
- **d.** Attachments can be files of any type, such as documents, spreadsheets, video, images, and sound files.

15. Which of the following is *not* in the message header?
- **a.** Mail subject
- **b.** All To recipients and Cc recipients
- **c.** Date and time the message was sent
- **d.** First three lines of the message body

16. To read a message that arrives in your Inbox, you _____.
- **a.** Click the Inbox header
- **b.** Double-click or click the message
- **c.** Click the Read button
- **d.** Flag the message to read

17. To send an attachment with your e-mail message, you _____.
- **a.** Click the Attach File or Attach button
- **b.** Drag the file into the message body
- **c.** Click Files, then click Insert
- **d.** You can't attach files to messages

18. When you forward a selected message to another person, the e-mail addresses for the original recipients of the message _____.
- **a.** Appear in the To text box
- **b.** Do not appear in any text box
- **c.** Appear in the Cc text box
- **d.** Appear in the To text box and the Cc text box

19. To create a new message, you _____.
- **a.** Click the Inbox button
- **b.** Click the Create button
- **c.** Click the New Mail Message button
- **d.** Click the Send button

20. To send the same message to multiple recipients, which of the following is *not* an option?
- **a.** Selecting multiple names from the address book
- **b.** Dragging the message to each of the recipient names in the address book
- **c.** Creating a distribution list containing the names of the recipients
- **d.** Entering multiple names in the To text box

▼ SKILLS REVIEW

1. **Start Outlook or your e-mail program and view the Inbox.**
   a. Start Outlook or your e-mail program.
   b. If necessary, select the mail client part of the program.
   c. Click the Send/Receive button or link to get new e-mail delivered to the Inbox, if necessary.
   d. Open the Inbox to view any new messages.

2. **Create and send a message.**
   a. Open a new message window.
   b. Click the To text box, then type a friend's e-mail address.
   c. Type your e-mail address in the Cc text box.
   d. Type **Travel Incentive Program (TIP)** as the Subject of the message.
   e. In the message body, type: **The Human Resources Department has approved the annual trip to Belgium as part of the Travel Incentive Program for sales. Congratulations.**
   f. Send the message.

3. **Manage e-mail folders.**
   a. Review the mail folders in your e-mail program.
   b. Look for a Sent Items or Sent folder and see if the Travel Incentive Program message is in that folder.
   c. Open the Deleted Items or Trash folder. See if any e-mail is in that folder.
   d. Review the Spam or Junk E-Mail folder.

4. **Receive and reply to a message.**
   a. If necessary, click the Send/Receive button to deliver messages to your Inbox.
   b. Display the contents of the Inbox folder.
   c. Open and read the message from yourself.
   d. Click the Reply button.
   e. In the message body, type **How exciting. What a great TIP! Belgium is a great place to send the employee with the most sales.**, then send the message.

5. **Forward a message.**
   a. Forward the message you received to another friend.
   b. In the top of the forwarded message body, type **I just wanted to close the loop on the travel incentive program. Belgium will be the destination this year.** (Refer to Figure A-16.)
   c. Send the message.
   d. Close the original message.

FIGURE A-16

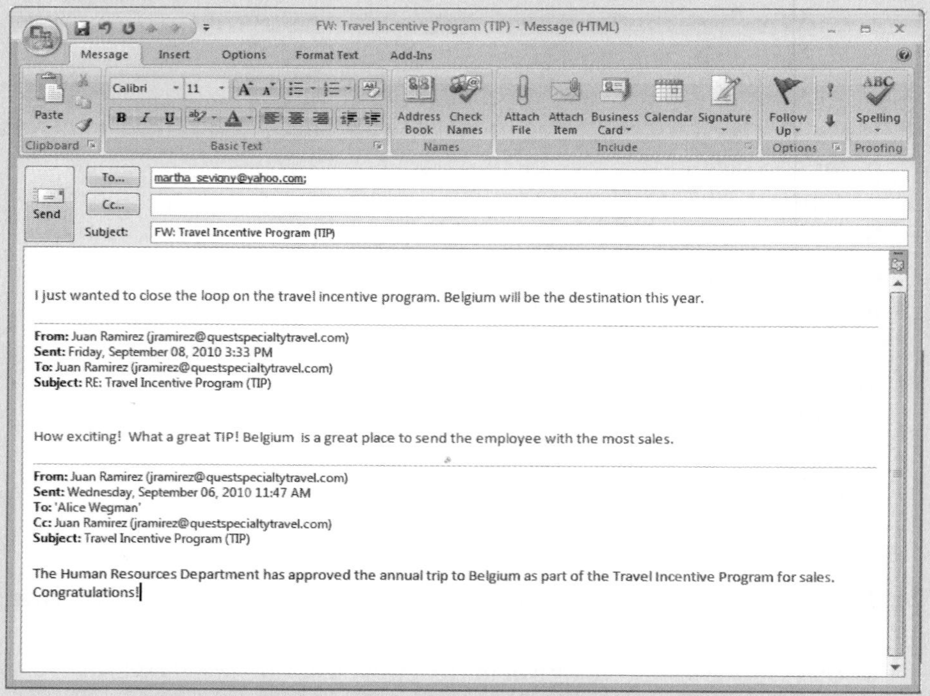

FW: Travel Incentive Program (TIP) - Message (HTML)

Message | Insert | Options | Format Text | Add-Ins

Calibri · 11 · A˙ A˙ | ≔ · ≔ · | B I U | aby · A · | ≡ ≡ ≡ | 年 年

Paste — Clipboard | Basic Text | Address Book Check Names — Names | Attach File Attach Item Business Card Calendar Signature — Include | Follow Up — Options | Spelling — Proofing

To... | martha_sevigny@yahoo.com;

Cc... |

Send

Subject: | FW: Travel Incentive Program (TIP)

I just wanted to close the loop on the travel incentive program. Belgium will be the destination this year.

From: Juan Ramirez (jramirez@questspecialtytravel.com)
Sent: Friday, September 08, 2010 3:33 PM
To: Juan Ramirez (jramirez@questspecialtytravel.com)
Subject: RE: Travel Incentive Program (TIP)

How exciting! What a great TIP! Belgium is a great place to send the employee with the most sales.

From: Juan Ramirez (jramirez@questspecialtytravel.com)
Sent: Wednesday, September 06, 2010 11:47 AM
To: 'Alice Wegman'
Cc: Juan Ramirez (jramirez@questspecialtytravel.com)
Subject: Travel Incentive Program (TIP)

The Human Resources Department has approved the annual trip to Belgium as part of the Travel Incentive Program for sales. Congratulations!

6. Send a message with an attachment.

    a. Create a new e-mail message.

    b. Enter your e-mail address as the message recipient.

    c. Enter your e-mail address in the Cc text box.

    d. Enter **Quest Logo** as the Subject of the message.

    e. In the message body, type: **Here is the logo you requested. Let me know if you need anything else.**

    f. Click the Insert File, Attach File, or Attach button or link.

    g. Navigate to the drive and folder where you store your Data Files.

    h. Select the file **QST Logo.jpg** (see Figure A-17), then click Insert, Open, or Attach (depending on your program).

FIGURE A-17

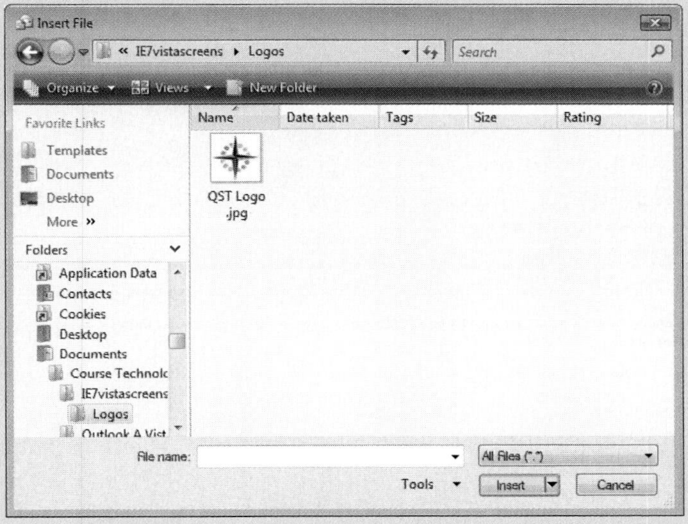

    i. Send the message.

7. Delete items.

    a. Delete all of the messages received in this exercise from the Inbox folder.

    b. Delete all of the messages sent in this exercise from the Sent Items folder.

    c. Empty the Deleted Items folder.

    d. Exit the e-mail program.

▼ INDEPENDENT CHALLENGE 1

You are a member of a planning board in your town. You have been appointed as the chairperson of the committee to investigate a proposal for rezoning a four-block area of downtown as open space. You decide to use e-mail to communicate with the other members of the committee as well as with the local newspaper, the town council, and the mayor.

a. Start Outlook or your e-mail program.

b. Open the address book and add yourself as well as three other new contacts to the address book. Use the names and e-mail addresses of classmates, teachers, or friends.

c. Create a new message and address it to yourself, then use the Cc field to send this message to two of the new contacts.

d. Type **Open space proposal — Public Hearing** as the Subject of the message.

e. In the message body, type **There will be a public hearing on Monday at 7:00 p.m. We should prepare our presentation and contact the local newspaper to be sure they carry the story.**

f. Press [Enter], then type your name. See Figure A-18.

FIGURE A-18

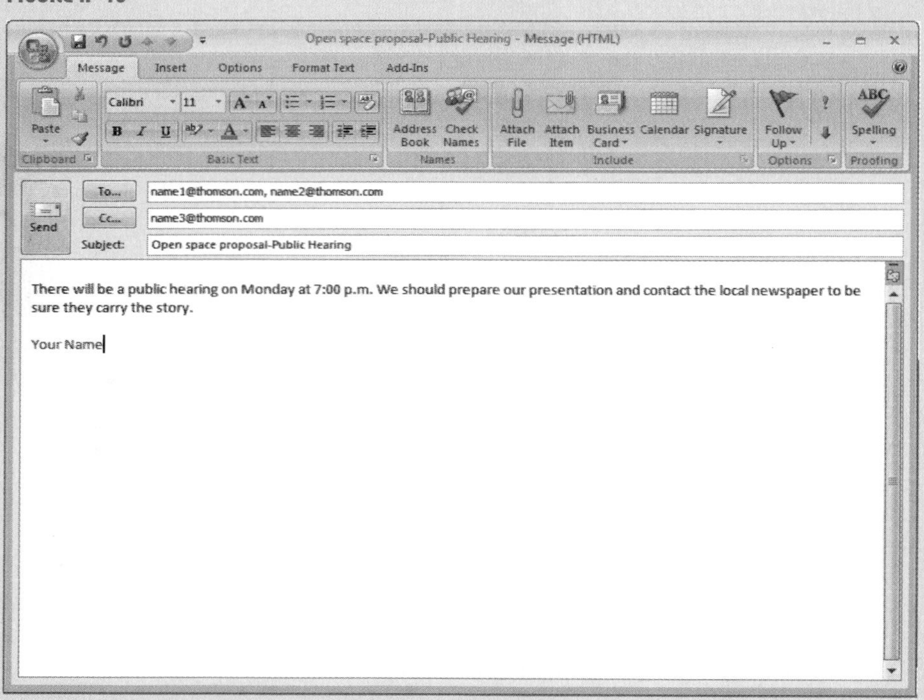

g. Send the message, then click the Send/Receive button if necessary. Depending on the speed and type of Internet connection you are using, you may need to click the Send/Receive button again, after waiting a few moments, if you do not receive the e-mail in your Inbox the first time you click the Send/Receive button.

h. Open the message in the Inbox, flag it with a follow-up flag or other symbol, then print it.

Advanced Challenge Exercise

■ Forward the message to the person you did not include in the distribution list.

■ In the message body, type: **Forgot to include you in this mailing! Please read the message; hope you can be there.**

■ Send the message.

i. Delete all of the messages related to this Independent Challenge from the Inbox folder.

j. Delete all of the messages related to this Independent Challenge from the Sent Items folder.

k. Delete the contacts that you added in this Independent Challenge from the Address Book.

l. Empty the Deleted Items folder.

m. Exit the e-mail program.

▼ INDEPENDENT CHALLENGE 2

You are planning a study trip to Africa with a group from the university. You have to send e-mail messages with an attachment as you organize this trip.

a. Start Outlook or your e-mail program, then create a new message and address it to two contacts, such as friends, family members, or classmates.

b. Enter your **e-mail address** in the Cc text box.

c. Type **Trip to Namibia** in the Subject text box.

d. Start your word processor and write a brief letter to your friends to encourage them to join you on the adventure. Conclude the document with a personal note about why you want to participate in a study program. Save the document file in the drive and folder where you store your Data Files, using a filename you will remember.

e. Type a short note in the message body of the e-mail to the recipients of the message, telling them that you thought they would like to join you on this trip, and that you are looking forward to them joining you.

f. Attach the word processing document to the message.

g. Send the message, then click the Send/Receive button. Depending on the speed and type of Internet connection you are using, you may need to click the Send/Receive button again, after waiting a few moments, if you do not receive a response e-mail the first time you click the Send/Receive button.

h. Print a copy of the message you receive in response.

Advanced Challenge Exercise

- Locate a picture or graphic image file on your computer that you want to send through e-mail.
- Right-click the picture, point to Send To, then click Mail Recipient on the shortcut menu. (Alternatively, after right-clicking a picture you may see these options: E-mail Picture or E-mail with [e-mail program]. These options will be different depending on your software and system.) Click OK if a dialog box opens asking if you want to make the picture smaller. Click Attach to attach the image to a new message window.
- When a new message window opens, enter your e-mail address in the To text box, then write a brief message in the body of the message.
- Send the message, then read the message and view the picture when it arrives in your Inbox.

i. Delete all of the messages received for this Independent Challenge from your Inbox.

j. Delete all of the messages sent for this Independent Challenge from the Sent Items folder.

k. Empty the Deleted Items folder.

l. Exit Outlook.

▼ VISUAL WORKSHOP

Refer to the e-mail message in Figure A-19 to complete this Visual Workshop. Use your e-mail program to create and then send this message. Be sure to send the message to at least one recipient. Attach a file that you created on your computer. It can be a document, worksheet, image, or database file.

FIGURE A-19

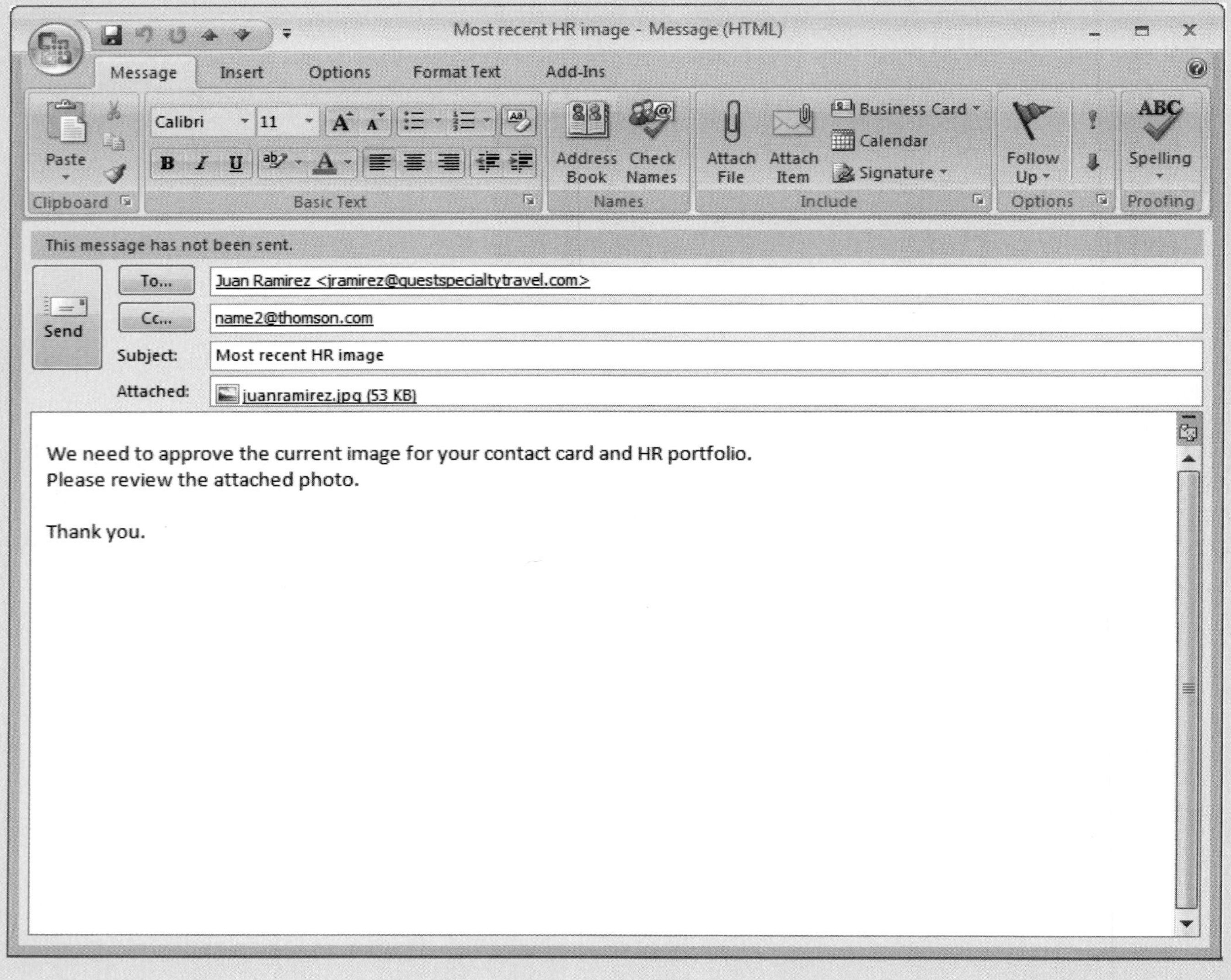

Managing Information Using Outlook

To effectively use Microsoft Office Outlook 2007 in managing your business and personal information, it is important to know not only how to send and receive e-mail, but also how to use the additional modules in Outlook. Outlook integrates several tools, including Mail, Calendar, Contacts, Tasks, Notes, and Journal, to provide you with a uniquely comprehensive information manager. Now that you know how to manage your e-mail, you will learn how Outlook acts as a desktop information manager to help you organize all aspects of your business and personal information.

OBJECTIVES

Start Outlook

Organize e-mail

Organize contacts

Manage appointments

Manage tasks

Create notes

Use the Journal

Apply categories

Starting Outlook

Outlook is a personal information and time management program that is part of the Microsoft Office 2007 suite. Outlook includes several components that work together: Mail, Contacts, Calendar, Tasks, Notes, and Journal. Outlook integrates these components so you can easily manage your schedule and information. The Outlook screen is fully customizable to let you view your contacts, schedule, or mail. The first time you start Outlook you will be prompted to set up a personal **account** that identifies you as a user. If you will be using Outlook for e-mail, you must enter information such as your e-mail address and password, the type of Internet service provider (ISP) you are using, and the incoming and outgoing mail server address for your ISP. More than one account can be set up in a single installation of Outlook. Each user has a username and password to gain access to his or her account. Accounts can be viewed by clicking Tools on the menu bar, then clicking Account Settings. To set up an account in Outlook for the first time, contact your technical resource person for the information you need. As the assistant to Juan Ramirez in the Human Resources department, you learn Outlook so you can use it for communication and scheduling. Refer to Figure B-1, which shows the Outlook Today window, as you read about how to customize the window.

STEPS

TROUBLE

If Outlook Today is not your default opening screen, click the Shortcuts shortcut in the Navigation Pane, then click Outlook Today on the Shortcuts list to view it.

1. **Click the Start button on the task bar, point to All Programs, click Microsoft Office, then click Microsoft Office Outlook 2007 to start Outlook**
    Outlook Today opens and shows your day at a glance, like an electronic version of a daily planner.

2. **Click View on the menu bar, point to Navigation Pane, then click Normal**
    The options on the View menu enable you to determine how the Navigation Pane, To-Do Bar, Reading Pane and toolbars appear in each of the Outlook modules. In Normal view, the **Navigation Pane** is open on the left side of the screen. In Mail view, it shows the Folder List. It has links and options for other views depending upon the module you are viewing, in addition to the navigation shortcuts. When minimized, the Navigation Pane is reduced to a vertical bar along the side of the Outlook window showing only the module navigation shortcuts.

QUICK TIP

Drag the border between the Folder List and shortcuts in the Navigation Pane to expand or shrink the list and minimize or maximize the shortcuts.

3. **Click View on the menu bar, point to To-Do Bar, then verify that there are checkmarks next to Normal, Date Navigator, Appointments, and Task List**
    The To-Do Bar, see Figure B-1, shows you what you need to do for the day. A calendar called the **Date Navigator** in the To-Do Bar gives you an overview of the month. You can mimimize the To-Do Bar so that it is reduced to a vertical bar on the right side of the window using the View menu, or by clicking the Minimize the To-Do Bar button next to the To-Do Bar Close button. You can also open the To-Do Bar Options dialog box, shown in Figure B-2, and adjust To-Do Bar display options. To open the To-Do Bar Options dialog box, click View on the menu bar, point to To-Do Bar, then click Options.

4. **Click View on the menu bar, point to Toolbars, then verify the checkmarks next to Standard and Web**

5. **Click View on the menu bar, then verify that there is a check mark next to Status Bar**

6. **Click Go on the menu bar, then review the options**
    Mail, Calendar, Contacts, Tasks, Notes, and Journal are the modules in Outlook. You can open any of these modules either by clicking the option on the Go menu or by clicking the shortcut in the Navigation Pane.

7. **Click Go on the menu bar, then click Shortcuts**
    The Navigation Pane now contains a list of shortcuts. You can customize the list to create a shortcut to any folder or group. Outlook Today is a default shortcut.

8. **Click Go on the menu bar, then click Folder List**
    The Folder List in the Navigation Pane displays each folder under Personal Folders with Outlook items specific to your account. See the example Folder List in Figure B-3.

FIGURE B-1: Outlook Today

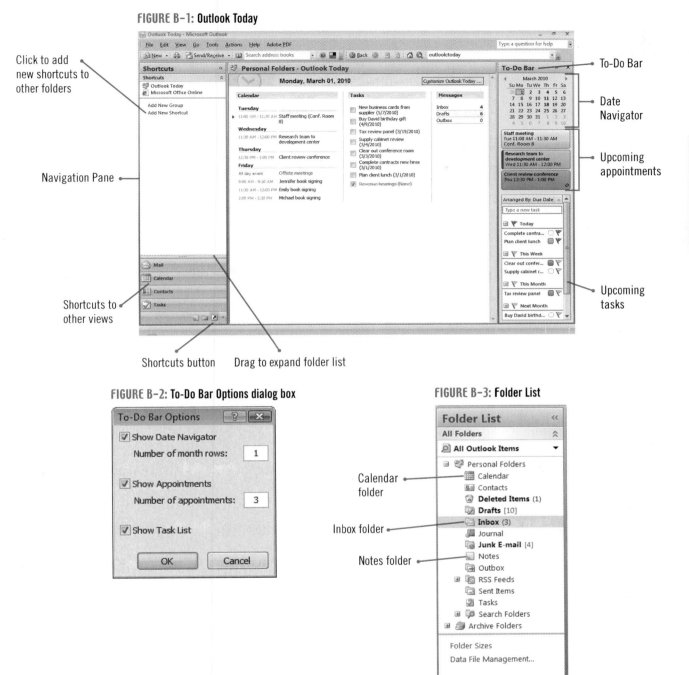

Click to add new shortcuts to other folders

To-Do Bar

Date Navigator

Navigation Pane

Upcoming appointments

Upcoming tasks

Shortcuts to other views

Shortcuts button

Drag to expand folder list

FIGURE B-2: To-Do Bar Options dialog box

To-Do Bar Options

☑ Show Date Navigator

Number of month rows: 1

☑ Show Appointments

Number of appointments: 3

☑ Show Task List

OK   Cancel

FIGURE B-3: Folder List

Folder List «

All Folders

All Outlook Items ▼

☐ Personal Folders
Calendar
Contacts
Deleted Items (1)
Drafts [10]
Inbox (3)
Journal
Junk E-mail [4]
Notes
Outbox
☐ RSS Feeds
Sent Items
Tasks
☐ Search Folders
☐ Archive Folders

Folder Sizes
Data File Management...

Calendar folder

Inbox folder

Notes folder

What is RSS?

The Internet has many Web sites that provide an overwhelming amount and variety of information. News sites are updated hourly; some corporations deliver news about products daily; there are entertainment Web sites that provide information about films and shows weekly; and many organizations keep their sites current. To stay on top of all this changing information, you would have to visit each site each day — a seemingly impossible task. Fortunately, there are technologies on the Internet that can help you stay current in topics that interest you. **Really Simple Syndication (RSS)** is a format for "feeding" or "syndicating" news or any content from Web sites to your computer. Outlook provides a way to have this information come directly into an RSS Feeds folder on your desktop. Access to RSS content is free, but you have to subscribe to a Web site that offers RSS feeds. RSS feeds provide subscribers with summaries that link to the full versions of the content. Once you see that you want to read more about the topic, you can click the link to view the article in the Reading Pane. You can organize the RSS feeds by creating folders for each topic or Web site that you subscribe to. The advantage to using RSS is that you may select different types of information from a variety of Web sites and view them all at the same time.

Organizing E-Mail

You have learned many basic features of creating and sending e-mail in any e-mail program, but using Outlook as your e-mail program enables you to take advantage of its features for organizing your e-mail, such as by color, view, or folder. The Inbox folder is where all new e-mail comes in unless you set up rules to deliver e-mail in other folders. A **rule** might specify that all e-mail from a certain person goes into the folder for a specific project. Outlook also has an active Junk E-mail filter that filters out messages that contain certain words. You can add keywords to the Junk E-mail filter to better manage the e-mail that comes into the Inbox. You will receive e-mail from clients as well as QST employees as you work with Juan Ramirez in the Human Resources department. You set up Outlook to manage the e-mail and learn the many organizational features that make Outlook an excellent personal information manager for your e-mail.

STEPS

1. **Drag the bar above the Mail shortcut in the Navigation Pane down to expand the Folder List, then click the Mail shortcut in the Navigation Pane**

   Outlook Mail is now the active module. You see a list of all Mail folders in the Navigation Pane, divided into sections. The Favorite Folders section contains shortcuts to folders that you use most often. The Mail Folders section shows all available folders, including the Inbox, Deleted Items, Drafts, Junk E-mail, Outbox, RSS Feeds, Sent Items, Search Folders, and Archive Folders. See Figure B-4.

   > **QUICK TIP**
   > The Inbox folder appears in both the Favorite Folders list and the Mail Folders list. You can select the folder from either list.

2. **Click the Inbox in the Mail Folders list in the Navigation Pane, click View on the menu bar, point to Reading Pane, then click Right, if necessary**

   The option chosen on the Reading Pane submenu determines where the Reading Pane appears in the window – in this case, on the right. If you have messages in your Inbox, you can use the Reading Pane to view a message without completely opening the message.

3. **Click Actions on the menu bar, point to Junk E-mail, then click Junk E-mail Options**

   The Junk E-mail Options dialog box opens, as shown in Figure B-5. You can specify different levels of junk e-mail protection in this dialog box to keep your Inbox free from spam.

4. **Click the Safe Senders tab, click the Safe Recipients tab, click the Blocked Senders tab, click the International tab, then click Cancel**

   There are many ways you can control the e-mail that you receive. By specifying safe senders and blocked senders, you can be sure that the e-mail you get is the e-mail you want to receive. For example, if you know someone is going to send you e-mail and you don't want the messages to be classified as junk e-mail, you can add that person's e-mail address to your Safe Senders list. If e-mail comes in that you know is offensive or junk, you can add the source address to the Blocked Senders list.

   > **QUICK TIP**
   > You can also click Arrange By in the Inbox column header, then, on the list that is displayed, click an option (such as Date) to sort the e-mail by that option.

5. **Click View on the menu bar, then point to Arrange By**

   You can determine how you view the e-mail in any folder. Options include by Date, Conversation, From, To, Categories, Flag, Size, Subject, Type, Attachments, E-mail Account, and Importance.

6. **Click View on the menu bar, point to Current View, then click Messages**

   You can use Outlook to quickly filter your e-mail based on specific criteria, such as who sent you a message or when you received a message.

7. **Click the New button on the Standard toolbar to open the new untitled Message window, as shown in Figure B-6**

8. **If you have set up an e-mail account, enter information into the To text box, the Subject text box, and body of the message, then click the Send button**

   Depending on how your e-mail is setup, a copy might be placed in the Outbox for later mailing. Once the message is sent, a copy of the message is placed in the Sent Items folder.

FIGURE B-4: Outlook Mail

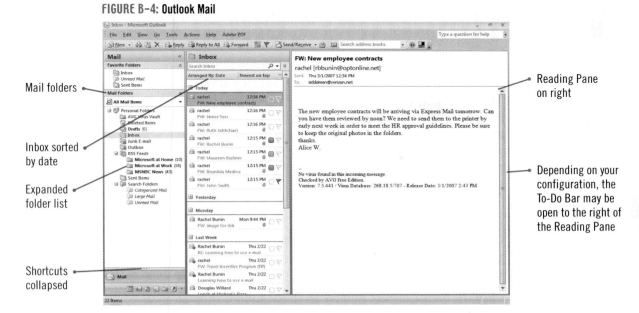

Mail folders

Inbox sorted by date

Expanded folder list

Shortcuts collapsed

Reading Pane on right

Depending on your configuration, the To-Do Bar may be open to the right of the Reading Pane

FIGURE B-5: Junk E-mail Options dialog box

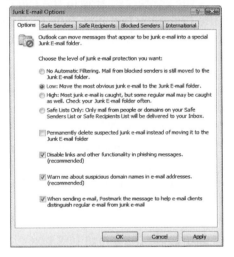

FIGURE B-6: New Message window

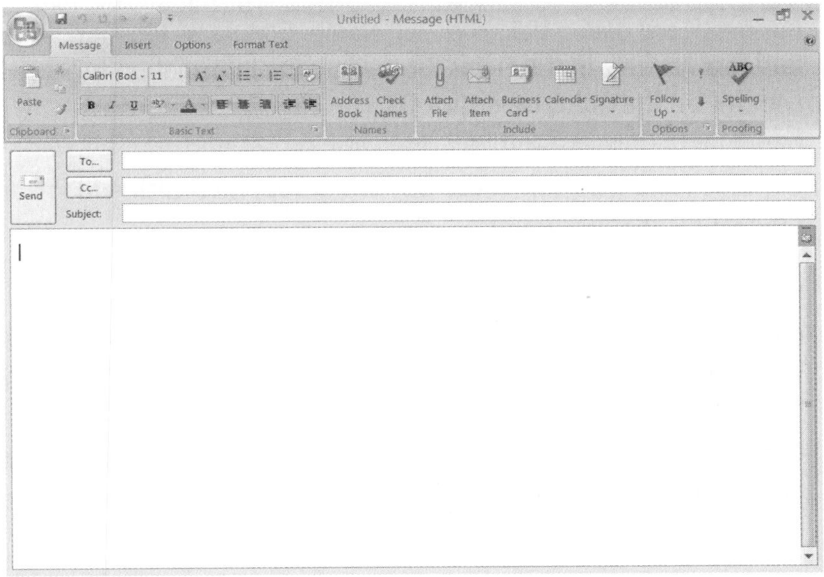

Organizing Contacts

Contacts in Microsoft Outlook enables you to manage all your business and personal contact information. When you create a contact for a person with whom you want to communicate, you store general and detailed information in fields for all Contacts in the Contacts folder. Each field, such as first name, stores specific information. Once you create a contact, you can use the Contacts features to do tasks such as the following: quickly address and send a letter, locate a phone number, make a call, send a meeting request, or e-mail a message. You can sort, group, and filter contacts by any field. You can also easily share contacts within your business or personal community. ▨▨▨▨ You learn about Contacts so you can store all the contact information for employees in Outlook.

STEPS

1. **Click the Contacts shortcut in the Navigation Pane**

   The Navigation Pane changes to Contacts view. You can click an option button in the Current view section to change how you view contacts.

2. **Click the New Contact button on the Standard toolbar**

   See Figure B-7. You enter information for a new contact in each field in the Contact window.

   QUICK TIP
   All fields do not have to be complete in a Contact card.

3. **Type your name as the contact's name in the Full Name text box, type Quest Specialty Travel (QST) in the Company text box, type Human Resources Assistant in the Job title text box, then type your Business, Home, and Mobile telephone numbers in the appropriate text boxes**

   If you do not enter a first and last name in the Full Name text box, the Check Full Name dialog box opens so you can enter the full name for the contact, including title, first name, middle name, last name, and suffix. You can click the File as list arrow in the Contact window to choose from several File as options. Outlook allows you to file each contact under different formats, including by first name, last name, company, or job title.

4. **Click the Addresses list arrow, click Business if necessary, click the This is the mailing address check box, then type your address in the Address text box**

   You can store up to three addresses in the Address text box. Choose Business, Home, or Other from the Addresses list, then type the address in the Address text box. If Outlook can't identify an address component that you type in the Address text box, the Check Address dialog box opens for you to verify it.

5. **Type your e-mail address in the E-mail text box**

   You can store up to three e-mail addresses for each contact.

   QUICK TIP
   Click the Add button or the Remove button under the Fields list in the dialog box to add or remove fields to or from the business card.

6. **Click the Business Card button in the Options group on the Ribbon to open the Edit Business Card dialog box, click Full Name, Company, Job Title, Business Phone, and Business Address in the Fields list to view the information for each field in the Edit window on the right, then click OK**

   You use the Edit Business Card dialog box to view and edit, when necessary, contact information.

7. **Click the Picture button in the Options group, then click Add Picture to open the Add Contact Picture dialog box**

   You use the Add Contact Picture dialog box to navigate to the drive and folder where the photo is stored, select the photo, and then click Open.

   QUICK TIP
   When you create a new Outlook item, such as a task, appointment, phone call, or note, you can link it to the contact or contacts to which it relates.

8. **Click Cancel, then click the Details button in the Show group on the Ribbon**

   You can enter a contact's detailed information, including the contact's department, profession, assistant's name, the contact's birthday, anniversary, spouse or partner's name, or even the contact's nickname.

9. **Click the General button in the Show group on the Ribbon, then click the Save & Close button in the Actions group to save and close the contact**

   Figure B-8 shows a completed contact with a business card.

FIGURE B-7: **New Contact window**

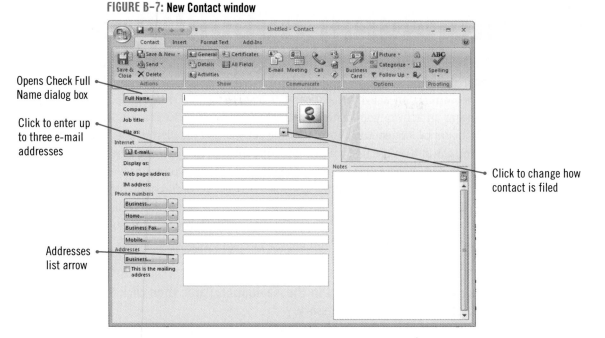

Opens Check Full Name dialog box

Click to enter up to three e-mail addresses

Addresses list arrow

Click to change how contact is filed

FIGURE B-8: **Completed Contact**

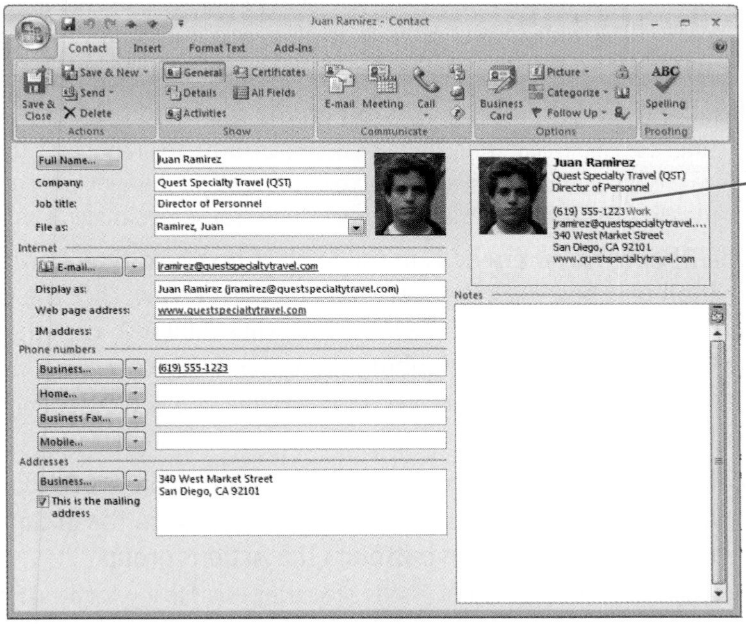

Business card generated based on contact information

Create a mailing list

You can create a subset of your Contacts folder by filtering the Contacts list. When you **filter** a list, you search for only specific information—for example, only those contacts that live in New Jersey. Using this filtered list and mail merge, you can use Outlook to create a variety of merged documents in Word, such as form letters or mailing labels. You can also use a filtered list and mail merge to send bulk e-mail messages or faxes to your contacts. To filter contacts, click Contacts in the Navigation Pane, click the Customize Current View link in the Navigation Pane to

open the Customize View dialog box. Click Filter to open the Filter dialog box, specify the filter criteria, then click OK. Once you have filtered the contacts you want for the merge, click Tools on the menu bar, then click Mail Merge to start the merge. Complete the Mail Merge Contacts dialog box to specify the contacts, fields, and document file to use, and to designate merge options such as document type and whether you want to merge to a new document, a printer, or e-mail.

Managing Appointments

The **Calendar** in Microsoft Outlook provides a convenient, effective way to manage your appointments. Calendar is the electronic equivalent of your desk calendar or pocket calendar. Calendar defines an **appointment** as an activity that does not involve inviting other people or scheduling resources, a **meeting** as an activity you invite people to or reserve resources for, and an **event** as an activity that lasts 24 hours or longer. You can specify the subject and location of the activity and its start and end times. You can also ensure that you do not forget the activity by having Outlook sound a reminder for you prior to the start of the activity. When you create an activity, Outlook notifies you if the new activity conflicts with, or is adjacent to, another scheduled activity. Recurring appointments or events can be set by specifying the recurrence, such as every week, month, or any period of time, and when the recurrence ends. You can view any period of time in Calendar. You will use Outlook to manage the schedule of appointments for Juan Ramirez and the Human Resources department.

STEPS

1. **Click the Calendar shortcut in the Navigation Pane, then click the Week button at the top of the Calendar if necessary**

   The Calendar, as shown in Figure B-9, can be viewed either by day, week, or month. The To-Do Bar, if open, shows the current month in the Date Navigator; if the To-Do Bar is closed, the Date Navigator appears in the Navigation Pane. You can use the Date Navigator in the To-Do Bar or Navigation Pane to quickly view specific dates. Dates with appointments or events appear in bold in the Date Navigator. Tasks for each day appear below the Calendar so you can see what tasks are due on each day.

   > **QUICK TIP**
   >
   > To quickly enter an appointment, click the time slot in the Calendar, then type the information directly into it.

2. **Click the New Appointment button on the Standard toolbar**

   An untitled Appointment window opens. See Figure B-10. You can specify the subject and location, and categorize the appointment with a specific color to highlight the appointment type. Recurring appointments are entered once, then you set a recurrence pattern. These appointments are marked by a special indicator.

   > **QUICK TIP**
   >
   > When viewing the Calendar, if you click a meeting or appointment, the details appear in the Reading Pane.

3. **Type Review Travel Agendas in the Subject text box, type Conference Room A in the Location text box, click the Start time date list arrow, click the date that is one week from now, click the Start time list arrow, click 9:00 AM, click the Reminder list arrow in the Options group on the Ribbon, then click 1 day**

   If this were a one-time meeting, you could click the Save & Close button in the Actions group and the appointment would be set.

4. **Click the Recurrence button in the Options group on the Ribbon, review the default options, click the End after option button, type 52 in the occurrences text box, click OK, then click the Save & Close button in the Actions group**

   The appointment window closes. This is a recurring event that you attend for at least one year.

5. **Click the Day button at the top of the Calendar, click the Week button, then click the Forward button ⊙ next to the date three times**

   You can view the Calendar by day, week, or month. When you view the calendar by week, you click the Show work week option button at the top of the Calendar to show Monday through Friday only, or you click the Show full week option button to show Sunday through Saturday. In all Calendar views, click the Show As list arrow to set a color bar to the left of the entry to identify the calendar time of the meeting or appointment as Free, Tentative, Busy, or Out of the Office.

6. **Click the Go to Today button on the Standard toolbar to return to today in the Calendar**

7. **Click the New list arrow on the Standard toolbar, then click Meeting Request**

   The Calendar can check the availability of all the invitees and resources for the meetings you want to set up.

8. **Click the Cancel Invitation button in the Actions group on the Meeting tab, close the untitled Appointment window, then click No to saving changes, if necessary**

FIGURE B-9: Calendar for a week

Today

Appointment

Selected week

Click to scroll months

Date Navigator

All day event

Recurring Appointment

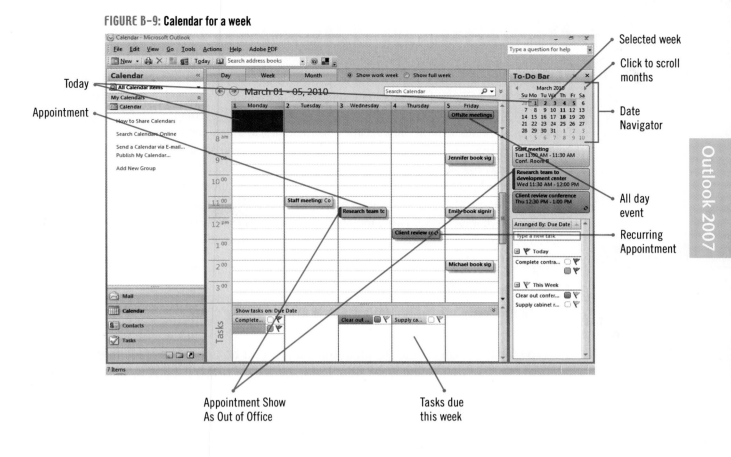

Appointment Show As Out of Office

Tasks due this week

FIGURE B-10: New Appointment window

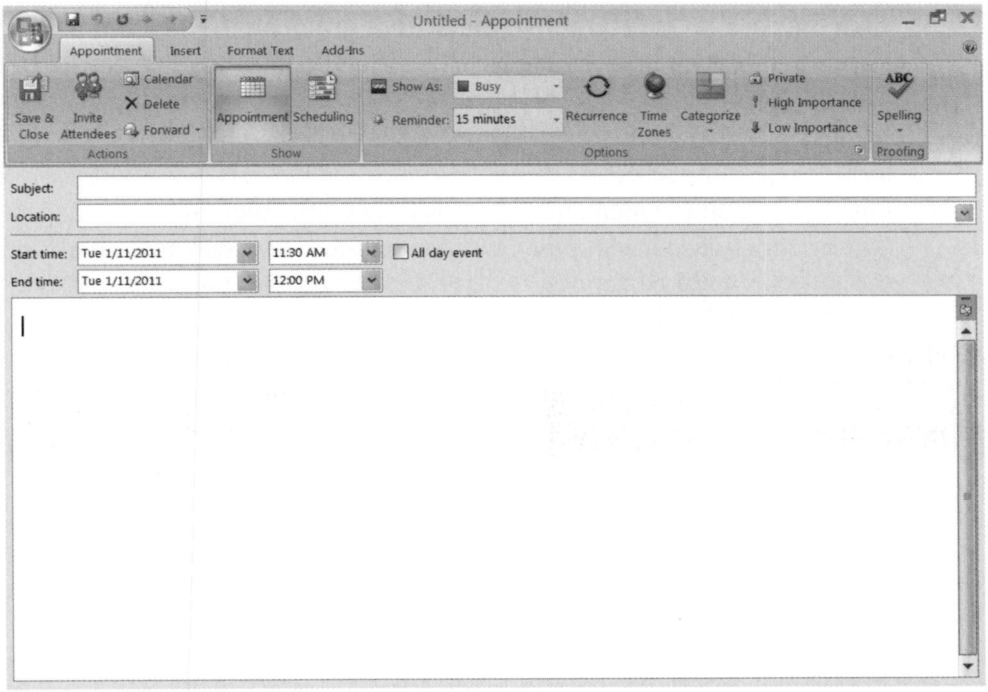

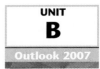

Managing Tasks

Tasks is an Outlook module that is an electronic to-do list. When you have something that has to be done, you can enter it in Tasks. Each task has a subject, a start and due date, and a description. You can also assign a priority to a task. You can mark your progress on tasks by percentage complete, and you can have Outlook create status summary reports in e-mail messages, and then send the summary to anyone on an update list for the task. Tasks can also have reminders. When you are in an Outlook module other than Tasks, your tasks appear at the bottom of the To-Do Bar, if it is open. You can also view the tasks that are due on each date in the Calendar. Similar to meetings and events, tasks can recur. You can also assign a flag and category to each task to help you organize your tasks. ▄▄▄▄ You always have many tasks that are due as part of your job. A week from tomorrow, the main conference room at the office is being painted, and you have to prepare the room. You enter the task in Outlook to keep track of it.

STEPS

1. **Click the** Tasks shortcut **in the Navigation Pane**

2. **Click the** New Task button **on the Standard toolbar**
   The new untitled Task window opens.

3. **Type** Clear out conference room **in the Subject text box, click the** Start date list arrow, **click the** date **that is one week from today, click the** Priority list arrow, **click High, click the** Reminder check box, **click the** Reminder date list arrow, **then click the** date **that is one week from yesterday**

4. **Click the** Categorize button **in the Options group on the Task tab, click** Purple Category **(or the category that is purple, if it has a different name), click** No **in the Rename Category text box if necessary, click the** Follow Up button **in the Options group, then click** Next Week
   The completed task looks like Figure B-11.

QUICK TIP
You can also quickly enter a task by typing in the fields at the top of the To-Do List.

5. **Click the** Save & Close button **in the Actions group on the Task tab**
   You can sort your tasks in several different ways, such as by To-Do Title, Due Date, or Flag Status, by clicking a column header in the task list. Tasks can also be viewed in many ways by clicking the option buttons in the Navigation Pane. Figure B-12 shows Tasks in Simple List view. A few existing tasks appear in the window (your screen may be different).

6. **Click** Actions **on the menu bar, then click** New Task Request
   You can assign tasks to another person and have Outlook automatically update you on the status of the task completion. To assign a task, you fill in the e-mail address of the person to whom you are assigning the task, complete the task details, and then click Send.

7. **Click the** Cancel Assignment button **in the Manage Task group on the Task tab, close the untitled Task window, then click** No **to saving changes, if necessary**

TROUBLE
If the To-Do Bar is not open, click View on the menu bar, click To-Do Bar, then click Normal.

8. **Click the** Calendar shortcut **in the Navigation Pane, click the** Go to Today button **if the calendar does not open to today, then scroll to next week in the Calendar or Date Navigator or until you see the new task you just entered**
   To coordinate your tasks and your appointments, the task list from Tasks is displayed in the Tasks section below the Calendar. The task you just created should appear under the Calendar for next week. You can specify how tasks are organized in the To-Do Bar.

9. **Click the** Arranged By button **above the tasks in the To-Do Bar, then click** Start Date, **if necessary**
   To schedule time to complete a task, simply drag a task from the To-Do Bar to a time block in the Calendar. Any changes you make to a task are reflected in both the To-Do Bar in Calendar and the task list in Tasks.

FIGURE B-11: Task information entered

Purple category

Start and due dates

Reminder is set

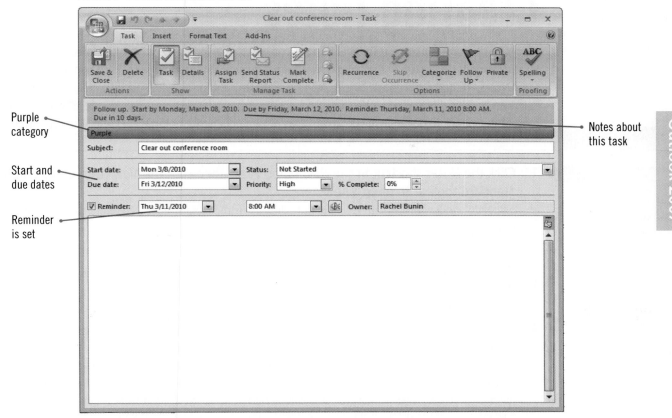

Notes about this task

FIGURE B-12: Tasks in Simple List view

Click to enter a new task

Tasks grouped by date due

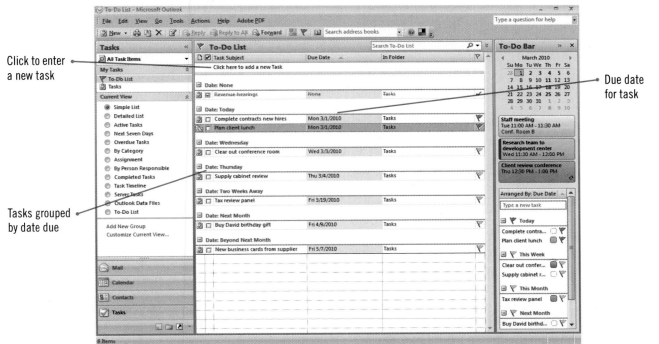

Due date for task

Creating Notes

Notes in Microsoft Outlook is the electronic version of the sticky notes or Post-It™ notes you buy at your local stationery store. Notes created in Outlook are a convenient way to quickly jot down a reminder or an idea. Notes, like tasks and appointments, can be organized and grouped by having categories, contacts, or colors assigned to them. You can also forward a note to share an idea with a colleague. You use Notes module in Outlook to quickly write down an idea concerning a new employee at Quest Specialty Travel.

STEPS

QUICK TIP

If a note is covering an area of the window you want to view, click the title bar of the note and drag it to a new location.

1. **Click the Notes shortcut in the Navigation Pane, then click the New Note button on the Standard toolbar to open a new note**

   The Note window opens. You type the note directly in the Note window. The note should begin with a meaningful phrase so that the Notes list displays a clear descriptive title for it.

2. **Type Jennifer Michaels-File new health benefit forms with insurance company**

3. **Click the Note icon in the upper-left corner of the Note window to open a menu**

   You can color-code each note, assign a contact to the note, and forward or print the note. Notes are date and time stamped at the time they are created.

4. **Point to Categorize, then click Purple Category (or the name of the purple category, if necessary)**

   Figure B-13 shows the new note. The Navigation Pane provides many options for viewing the Notes in order to organize them the way you want. If you want to turn a note into an appointment or meeting, you drag the note from the Notes window to the Calendar button in the Navigation Pane. A new appointment window opens with the details from the note filled in the appropriate fields. If you drag the note to the Tasks button in the Navigation Pane, a new task window opens and you can specify a due date and other details.

5. **Close the note**

Sending Business Cards or VCards

You can send contact information over the Internet easily with Outlook. If you know someone has Outlook 2007, you can send a contact business card. In Contacts view, click the contact you want to send, click Actions on the menu bar, then click Send as Business Card. **VCards** are the Internet standard for creating and sharing virtual business cards. To send a vCard to someone via e-mail, click the contact you want to send as a vCard, click Actions on the menu bar, point to Send Full Contact, then click In Internet Format (vCard). You can also include your vCard with your e-mail signature.

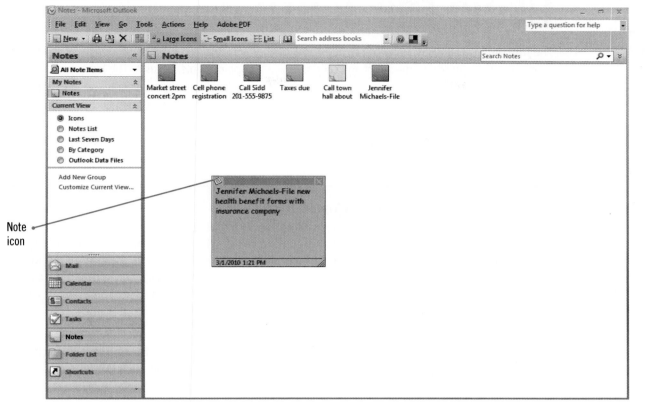

Note icon

Customizing Outlook Today

When Outlook Today is open, you can see what is happening in the Calendar, Tasks, and Messages for the day. Outlook Today shows your appointments over a range of time in the Calendar section. It also displays your tasks in one convenient place. In the Customize Outlook Today pane, you can decide to go directly to Outlook Today when Outlook opens, if it does not open automatically. You can also choose to show from one to seven days of appointments in the Calendar section, and you can sort your tasks in Outlook Today by Importance, Due Date, Creation Time, or Start Date, and in ascending or descending order. If you use Outlook for e-mail, Outlook Today displays how many messages are in your Inbox, Outbox, and Drafts folders. You can also add or delete folders from the Messages folder list. To customize Outlook Today, view the Outlook Today page, click the Customize Outlook Today link to the right of the date in Outlook Today and customize the information that appears to fit your personal style and work habits. Pick a different visual appearance for Outlook Today from an available list. Click the Save Changes button in the Customize Outlook Today pane to save any changes you make

Using the Journal

The **Journal** in Outlook is a way to provide a trail of your activities within Microsoft Office. If you turn the Journal on, you can see a timeline of any calls, messages, appointments, or tasks. The Journal also tracks all documents, spreadsheets, databases, presentations, or any Office file that you specify. The Journal may not have been on when you created a spreadsheet or document that you want to be recorded in the Journal. Use Windows Explorer or the desktop to locate the file or item you want to record, then drag the item to the Journal and select the options you want for the entry. 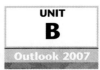 You use the Journal to help assign documents to contacts.

STEPS

1. **Click Go on the menu bar, click Journal, then click Yes**

   To turn on the Journal, you specify the Journal options, such as which items to track, in the Journal Options dialog box, shown in Figure B-14. The Journal is displayed as a timeline on your screen. Any activities that have been specified to be tracked appear for each day as icons. You can scroll through the Journal to get an overview of your activities. You can sort or group the activities in the Journal. If you want to recall an event, the Journal is a great tool; you can see any documents that may have been created on a specific day. The Journal folder contains shortcuts to the activities that have been recorded.

2. **Click the E-mail message check box in the Automatically record these items box, click the check box next to your name in the For these contacts list, then click OK**

3. **Click the Mail shortcut in the Navigator Pane, click the New Mail Message button on the Standard toolbar, then send yourself a test message**

4. **Click Go on the menu bar, click Journal, then review the Journal entry, as shown in Figure B-15**

5. **Click Tools on the menu bar, click Options to open the Options dialog box, then click Journal Options in the Contacts and Notes section of the dialog box**

   You can remove, add, or change Journal options at any time by working in the Journal Options dialog box.

6. **Click to remove the check marks from the E-mail Message check box and from your contact name**

7. **Click OK to close the Journal Options dialog box, then click OK to close the Options dialog box**

FIGURE B-14: Journal Options dialog box

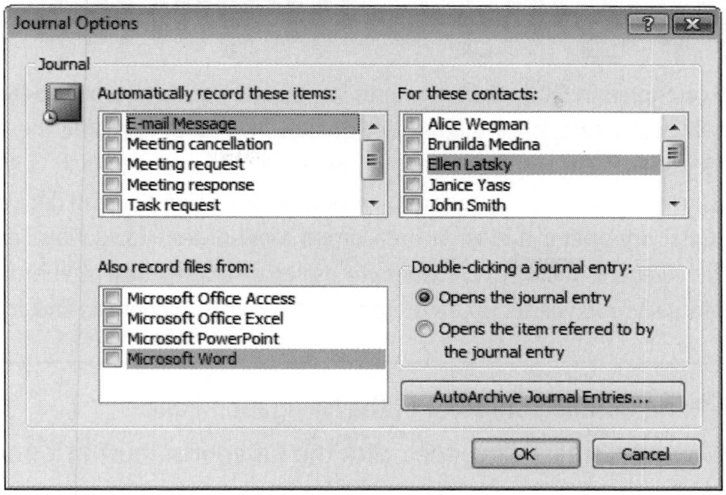

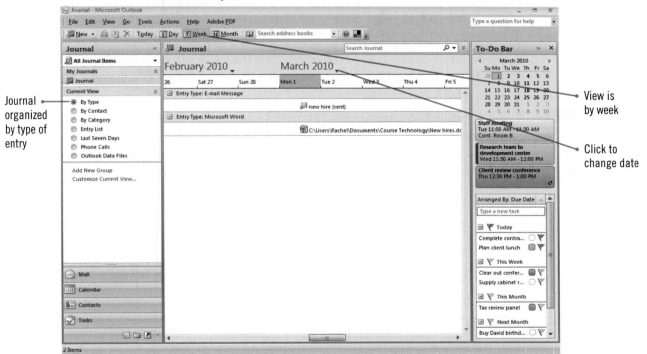

FIGURE B-15: Recorded Journal entry

Journal organized by type of entry

View is by week

Click to change date

Applying Categories

You use categories in Outlook to tag items so you can track and organize them by specific criteria. Outlook comes with color categories that are set by default. You can rename the colors as needed. By assigning color categories to contacts, tasks, appointments, notes, or any item in Outlook, you can quickly review all items assigned to a specific category by reviewing the color. You can filter or sort by category. If you click the By Category option button in the Current View of the Navigation Pane, you can see your contacts clearly by category. QST wants to use color to help organize information about its contacts and staff. Eventually, you will set up a system to assign colors to contacts and staff based on region.

STEPS

1. **Click the Contacts shortcut in the Navigation Pane**

2. **Click your Contact card, then click the Categorize button ⊞ on the Standard toolbar**
   Outlook comes with six predefined color categories: Purple, Blue, Green, Orange, Red, and Yellow.

3. **Click Purple Category (or the name of the purple category, if necessary)**
   Your contact card is now assigned the color purple.

4. **Click the Calendar shortcut in the Navigation Pane, scroll to next week, click the Review Travel Agendas appointment, click the Categorize button ⊞ on the Standard toolbar, then click Purple Category (or the category's name)**
   The appointment is also assigned the color purple.

5. **Click the Contacts shortcut in the Navigation Pane, then click the By Category option button in the Current View section of the Navigation Pane**
   The contacts are grouped by category, as shown in Figure B-16. You can rename categories to be meaningful while retaining the color coding.

6. **Make sure a contact card is selected, click the Categorize button ⊞ on the Standard toolbar, then click All Categories to open the Color Categories dialog box, as shown in Figure B-17**

QUICK TIP
If you are working on a shared computer, such as in a lab setting, repeat steps 6 and 7 to change the category name back to Purple Category.

7. **Click Purple Category (or the category's name), click Rename, type HR Assistant as the new name, then click OK**
   The name of the purple category changes to "HR Assistant" in the list of contacts by category. As you work on other applications at your computer, you can leave Outlook open so you can refer to your contacts, be reminded of appointments, and track entries in the Journal. However, at the end of the day, it is good practice to close all applications and shut down the computer.

8. **Click File on the menu bar, then click Exit to exit Outlook**

Coordinating calendars

The Calendar can check the availability of all the people and resources for the meetings you want to set up.

Once you select a meeting time and location, you can send invitations in meeting requests by entering contact names in the To text box, then clicking the Send button. The meeting request arrives in the invitee's Inbox with buttons to Accept, Reject, or Request a change directly in the e-mail message. If an invitee accepts the invitation, a positive e-mail reply is sent back to you, and Outlook posts the meeting automatically to the invitee's calendar. If you share calendars through a network, you can click the Open a Shared Calendar link in the Navigation Pane to view the calendars of your colleagues. To send a copy of a time period in your calendar to someone through e-mail, click the Send a Calendar via E-mail link in the Navigation Pane, adjust the options in the Send a Calendar via E-mail dialog box, click OK, then address and send the e-mail.

FIGURE B-16: Contacts grouped by category

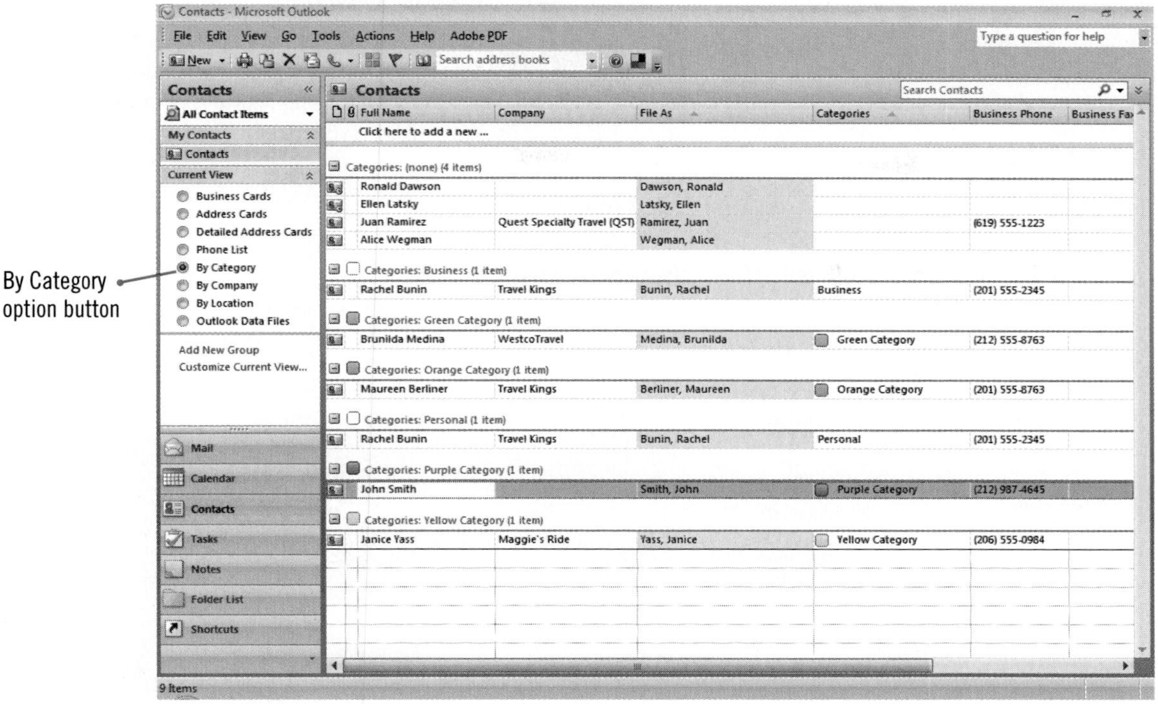

By Category
option button

FIGURE B-17: Color Categories dialog box

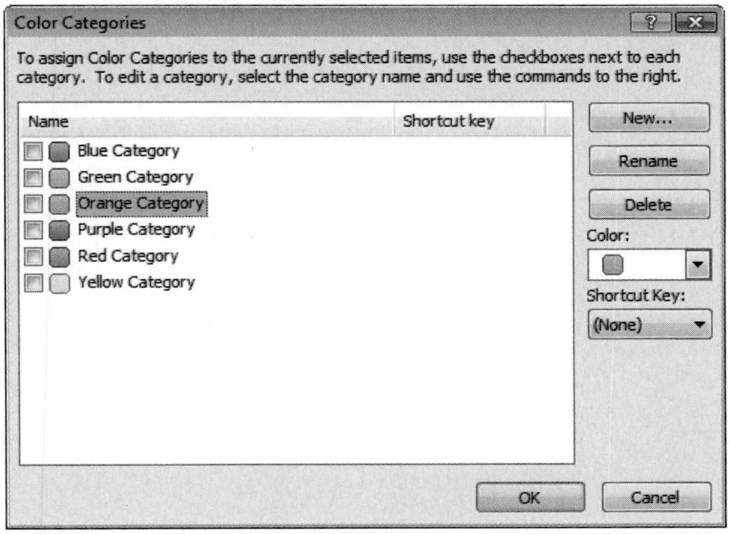

Practice

If you have a SAM user profile, you may have access to hands-on instruction, practice, and assessment of the skills covered in this unit. Log in to your SAM account (http://sam2007.course.com/) to launch any assigned training activities or exams that relate to the skills covered in this unit.

▼ CONCEPTS REVIEW

Label the elements of the Calendar window shown in Figure B-18.

FIGURE B-18

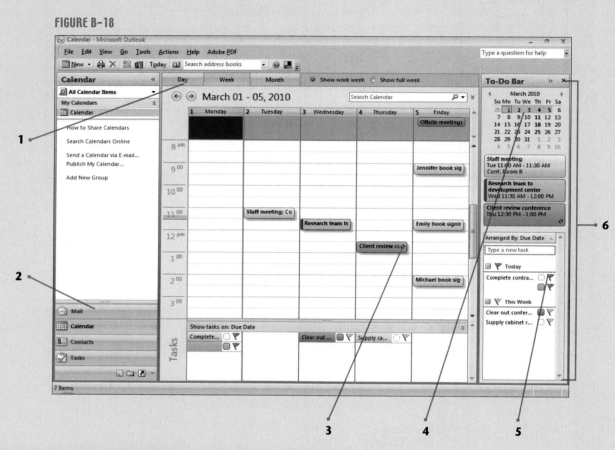

Match each term with the statement that best describes it.

7. **Notes**
8. **Tasks**
9. **E-mail**
10. **Calendar**
11. **Journal**

a. Track e-mail, documents, activities
b. Keep and track appointments
c. Jot down ideas or reminders
d. Manage a to-do list
e. Send and receive messages

Select the best answer from the list of choices.

12. Which of the following is *not* available in Outlook?
   a. Mail
   b. Notes
   c. Calendar
   d. Planner

13. To schedule your appointments, meetings, and events, you use _____.
   a. Tasks
   b. Notes
   c. Contacts
   d. Calendar

14. To manage your business and personal to-do list, you use _____.
   a. Tasks
   b. Journal
   c. Contacts
   d. Calendar

15. To track appointments, documents, and activities, you use _____.
   a. Tasks
   b. Journal
   c. Contacts
   d. Calendar

16. The difference between an appointment and an event is that _____.
   a. An event cannot recur
   b. An appointment lasts less than 12 hours
   c. An event lasts 24 hours or more
   d. You cannot categorize an event

17. Which of the following is *not* visible on the To-Do Bar?
   a. E-mail in the Inbox
   b. An appointment for today
   c. Tasks due today
   d. Date Navigator

▼ SKILLS REVIEW

1. Start Outlook.

a. Click the Start Button on the taskbar, then start Outlook.

b. Arrange the Outlook window so that the Navigation Pane is in Normal view and contains the folder list, and the To-Do Bar appears on the right side of the screen.

c. Open Mail, then expand the folder list so the Navigation Pane buttons are minimized at the bottom. See Figure B-19.

2. Organize E-mail.

a. View the Inbox.

b. Sort the e-mail in the Inbox by sender, then sort the e-mail in the Inbox by date, most recent on top.

c. Open the Junk E-mail Options dialog box, review the junk e-mail options on the system, then close the dialog box.

d. Open a new message window and write an e-mail message to your instructor or a friend. Include an address in the Cc box, then type **Study group plans** as the subject of the message. As the body of the message, enter a brief message. See Figure B-20.

e. Send the message.

3. Organize contacts.

a. Open Contacts.

b. Open a new untitled Contact window.

c. Create a new contact for a family member.

d. Save and close the contact.

FIGURE B-19

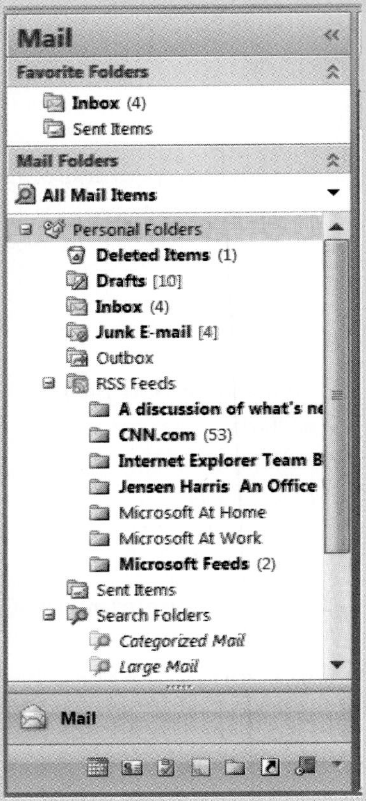

FIGURE B-20

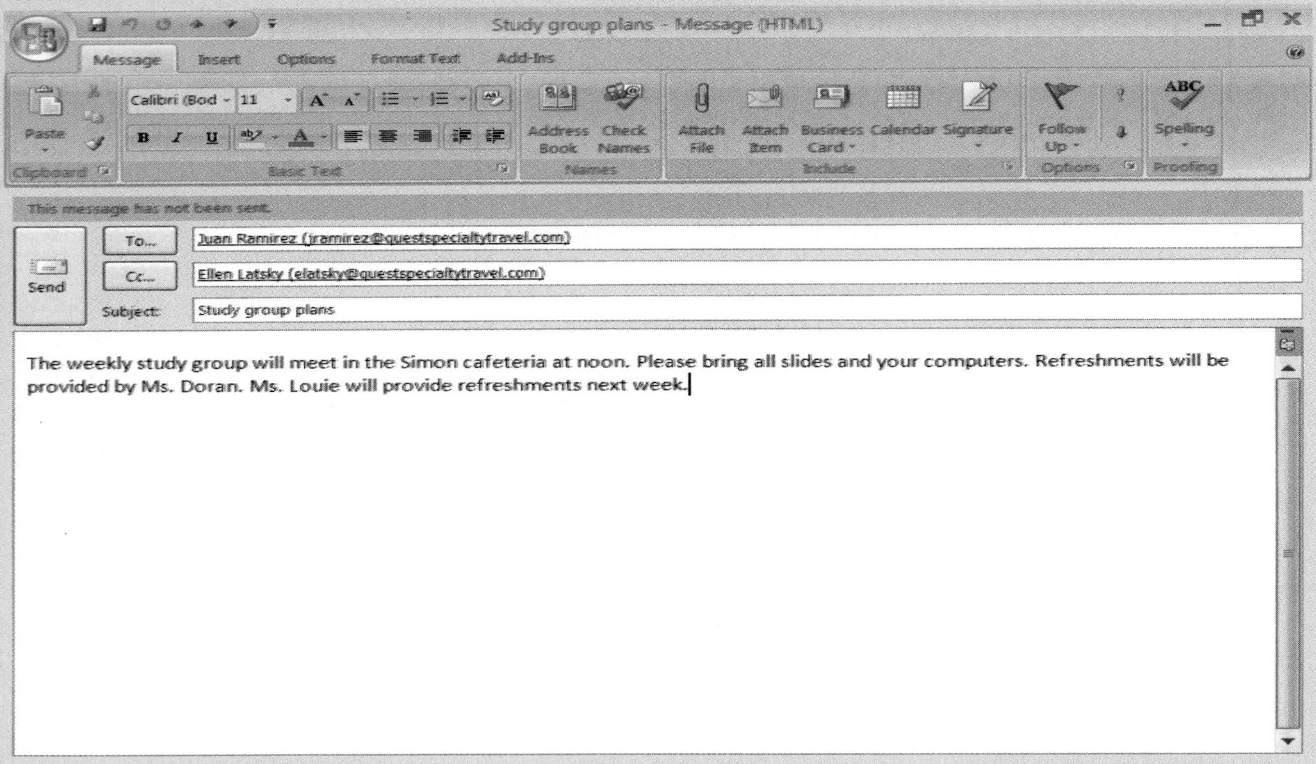

The weekly study group will meet in the Simon cafeteria at noon. Please bring all slides and your computers. Refreshments will be provided by Ms. Doran. Ms. Louie will provide refreshments next week.

▼ SKILLS REVIEW (CONTINUED)

4. Manage appointments.

- **a.** Open the Calendar.
- **b.** View the calendar by full week.
- **c.** View the calendar for today.
- **d.** Create a new appointment for next week for a two-and-a-half hour lunch meeting with Ruth, Maureen, and Janice at noon in the Stardust Diner.
- **e.** Set a reminder for two days ahead of the appointment. See Figure B-21.
- **f.** Save and close the appointment.

FIGURE B-21

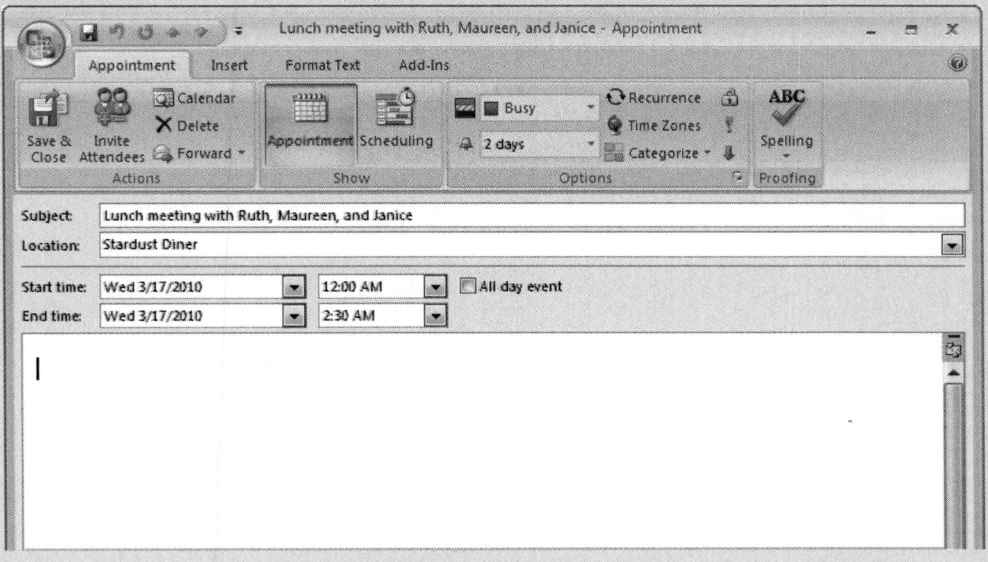

5. Manage tasks.

- **a.** Open Tasks.
- **b.** View the task list in Simple List and Detailed List views.
- **c.** Create a new task, due tomorrow, to buy your friend a birthday gift.
- **d.** Set a reminder for early morning. See Figure B-22.
- **e.** Save and close the task.

FIGURE B-22

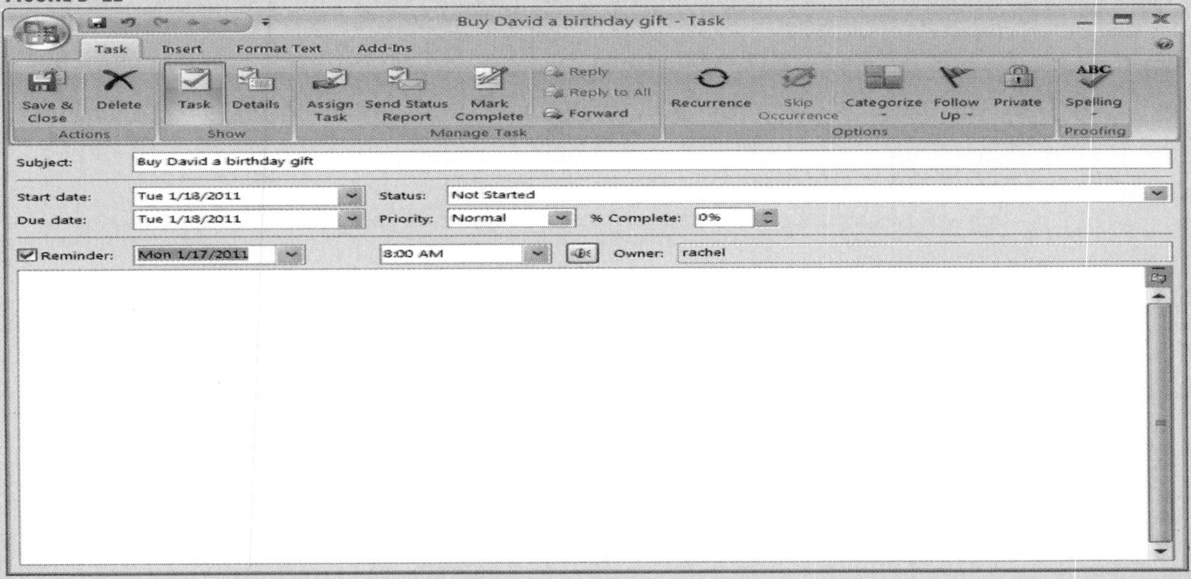

6. Create notes.

  a. Open Notes.

  b. Create a new note reminding you to call town hall about a new town ordinance.

  c. Categorize the note in the Red Category. See Figure B-23.

  d. Close the note.

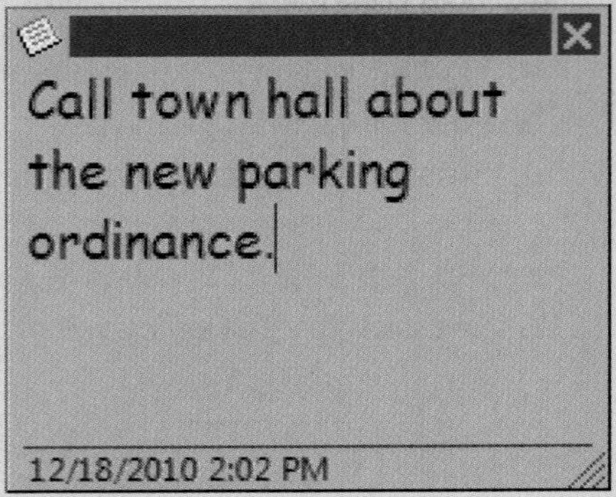

7. Use the Journal.

  a. Turn on the Journal.

  b. In the Journal Options dialog box, click the E-mail Message check box in the Automatically record these items box and the check box next to your own name in the For these contacts list to have the Journal track your e-mail messages.

  c. Send yourself an e-mail message.

  d. Click Go on the menu bar, then click Journal to view the Journal entry.

  e. Open the Journal Options dialog box, deselect the E-mail Message check box in the Automatically record these items box, then deselect the check box next to your name to turn tracking off.

  f. Close the Journal Options dialog box.

8. Apply categories.

  a. Open Contacts, then assign the Green Category to your Contact card.

  b. Assign a category to the lunch appointment that you created in Step 4.

  c. View Contacts by category. See Figure B-24.

  d. Exit Outlook.

FIGURE B-23

Call town hall about the new parking ordinance.

12/18/2010 2:02 PM

FIGURE B-24

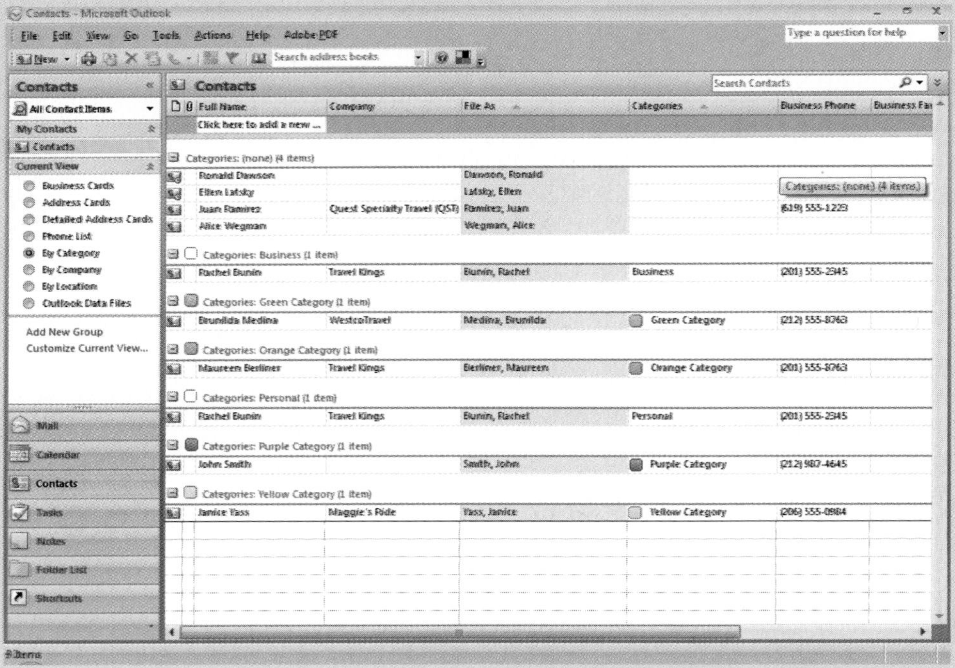

▼ INDEPENDENT CHALLENGE 1

As manager of a sporting goods store, your job is to develop a contact list of all customers that come in the store. The list will be used to send direct mail for future promotions. You created a form for each customer to complete so that you can gather their contact information. The contact information includes first and last name, mailing address, e-mail address, and at least one phone number. Each week you select one customer from the list of new names to receive a small prize package. You need to create the contact list in Outlook and use Outlook to schedule the weekly prize giveaway.

    a. Open Contacts in Outlook, and then create five new contact cards. Use your friends' information or make up fictitious names and contact information.

    b. Create two notes, each in the Purple category, that remind you of an event in the store.

    c. Create a recurring appointment on each Thursday for the next two months to select a winner from the list of new names.

    d. Enter two new tasks in the task list. One task is for you to review the employee compensation package, and the other task is for you to review the utility bills. Each task should have a start date of next week, a high priority, and be in the Yellow category.

    e. View the Calendar with the To-Do Bar open.

    f. Exit Outlook.

▼ INDEPENDENT CHALLENGE 2

Outlook is an integrated information management system that stores information in folders specific to the type of information stored. Outlook stores e-mail in Mail folders, Contacts in Contact folders, and so on. You can create new folders for specific types of information and view them in the folders list. You can also transfer one type of item to another, for example, you can drag a task to the Calendar to create an appointment. The integration of the different types of information is what makes Outlook so powerful. You are going to move items from one Outlook module to another to see how easily you can integrate information.

    a. Open Mail in Outlook, drag an e-mail message from the Inbox to the Tasks shortcut on the Navigation Pane, then, in a word processing document or on a piece of paper, explain what happens.

    b. Drag an e-mail message from the Inbox to the Notes shortcut in the Navigation Pane, then explain what happens.

    c. Open the Calendar, drag an existing appointment from the Calendar to the Tasks shortcut in the Navigation Pane, then explain what happens.

    d. Drag the same appointment to the Mail shortcut.

    e. View the Contacts list in Address Cards view. Drag a contact card from the Contacts list to the Calendar shortcut in the Navigation Pane, then explain what happens.

Advanced Challenge Exercise

    ■ Open a new appointment in Calendar, click the Categorize button in the Options group on the Ribbon, then click All Categories.

    ■ Rename the Purple category to a name of your choice.

    ■ Rename the Red category to a name of your choice. See Figure B-25.

    ■ Close the Color Categories dialog box, then close the appointment window.

    f. View the Contacts list in Business Cards view. Drag a contact card from the Contacts list to the Mail shortcut in the Navigation Pane, then explain what happens.

    g. Exit Outlook.

FIGURE B-25

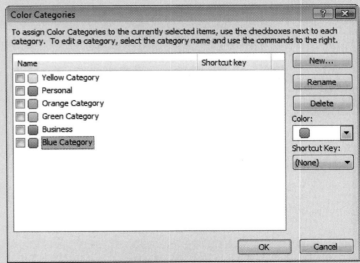

Start Outlook. First, create a note as shown in Figure B-26, then create an appointment as shown in Figure B-27, using a weekday in the next two weeks as the date for the appointment. Finally, using the same date as for the appointment, create a task as shown in Figure B-28. Note that the dates in the figures will differ from those on your screen.

FIGURE B-26

Simon Heller is the new manager at Dumont Office Supply on Main Street.

1/15/2010 12:54 PM

FIGURE B-27

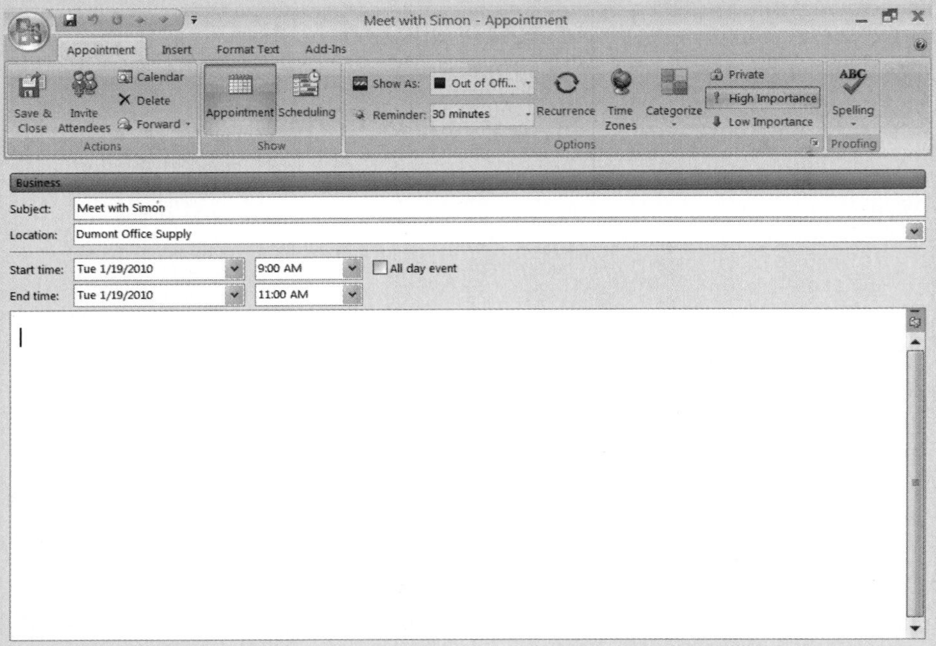

FIGURE B-28

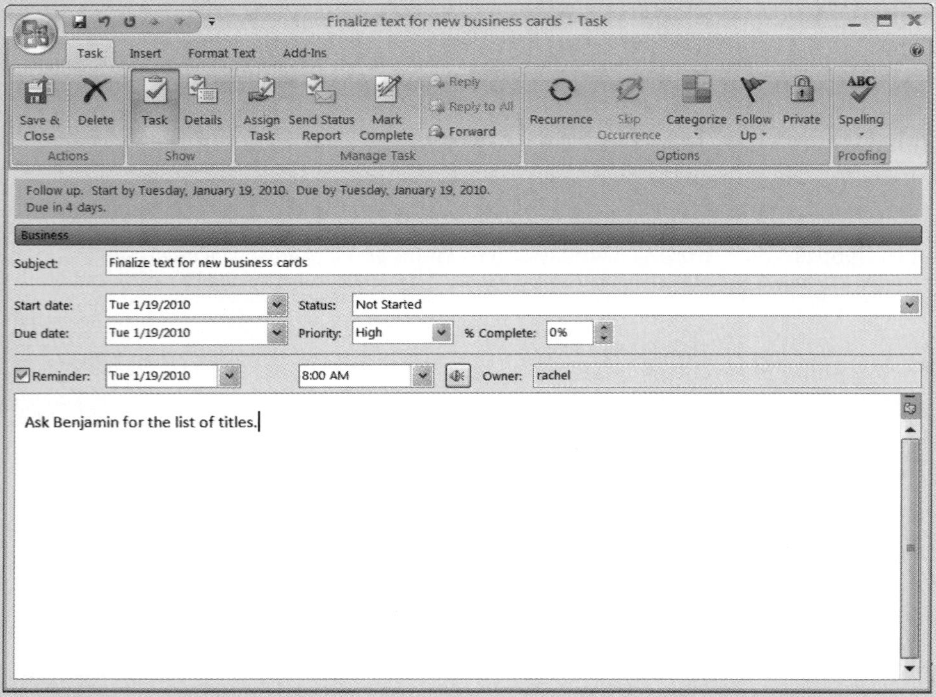

Appendix A
Appendix

Restoring Defaults in Windows Vista and Disabling and Enabling Windows Aero

Files You Will Need:

No files needed.

Windows Vista is the most recent version of the Windows operating system. An operating system controls the way you work with your computer, supervises running programs, and provides tools for completing your computing tasks. After surveying millions of computer users, Microsoft incorporated their suggestions to make Windows Vista secure, reliable, and easy to use. In fact, Windows Vista is considered the most secure version of Windows yet. Other improvements include a powerful new search feature that lets you quickly search for files and programs from the Start menu and most windows, tools that simplify accessing the Internet, especially with a wireless connection, and multimedia programs that let you enjoy, share, and organize music, photos, and recorded TV. Finally, Windows Vista offers lots of visual appeal with its transparent, three-dimensional design in the Aero experience. This appendix explains how to make sure you are using the Windows Vista default settings for appearance, personalization, security, hardware, and sound and to enable and disable Windows Aero. For more information on Windows Aero, go to *www.microsoft.com/windowsvista/experiences/aero.mspx*.

OBJECTIVES

Restore the defaults in the Appearance and Personalization section

Restore the defaults in the Security section

Restore the defaults in the Hardware and Sound section

Disable Windows Aero

Enable Windows Aero

Restoring the Defaults in the Appearance and Personalization Section

The following instructions require a default Windows Vista Ultimate installation and the student logged in with an Administrator account. All of the following settings can be changed by accessing the Control Panel.

- To restore the defaults in the Personalization section

  1. Click Start, and then click Control Panel. Click Appearance and Personalization, click Personalization, and then compare your screen to Figure A-1

  2. In the Personalization window, click Windows Color and Appearance, select the Default color, and then click OK

  3. In the Personalization window, click Mouse Pointers. In the Mouse Properties dialog box, on the Pointers tab, select Windows Aero (system scheme) in the Scheme drop-down list, and then click OK

  4. In the Personalization window, click Theme. Select Windows Vista from the Theme drop-down list, and then click OK

  5. In the Personalization window, click Display Settings. In the Display Settings dialog box, drag the Resolution bar to 1024 by 768 pixels, and then click OK

FIGURE A-1

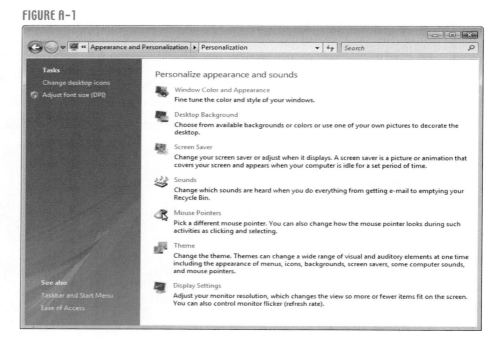

- To restore the defaults in the Taskbar and Start Menu section
  1. Click Start, and then click Control Panel. Click Appearance and Personalization, click Taskbar and Start Menu, and then compare your screen to Figure A-2
  2. In the Taskbar and Start Menu Properties dialog box, on the Taskbar tab, click to select all checkboxes except for "Auto-hide the taskbar"
  3. On the Start Menu tab, click to select the Start menu radio button and check all items in the Privacy section
  4. In the System icons section on the Notification Area tab, click to select all of the checkboxes except for "Power"
  5. On the Toolbars tab, click to select Quick Launch, none of the other items should be checked
  6. Click OK to close the Taskbar and Start Menu Properties dialog box

- To restore the defaults in the Folder Options section
  1. Click Start, and then click Control Panel. Click Appearance and Personalization, click Folder Options, and then compare your screen to Figure A-3
  2. In the Folder Options dialog box, on the General tab, click to select Show preview and filters in the Tasks section, click to select Open each folder in the same window in the Browse folders section, and click to select Double-click to open an item (single-click to select) in the Click items as follows section
  3. On the View tab, click the Reset Folders button, and then click Yes in the Folder views dialog box. Then click the Restore Defaults button
  4. On the Search tab, click the Restore Defaults button
  5. Click OK to close the Folder Options dialog box

- To restore the defaults in the Windows Sidebar Properties section
  1. Click Start, and then click Control Panel. Click Appearance and Personalization, click Windows Sidebar Properties, and then compare your screen to Figure A-4
  2. In the Windows Sidebar Properties dialog box, on the Sidebar tab, click to select Start Sidebar when Windows starts. In the Arrangement section, click to select Right, and then click to select 1 in the Display Sidebar on monitor drop-down list
  3. Click OK to close the Windows Sidebar Properties dialog box

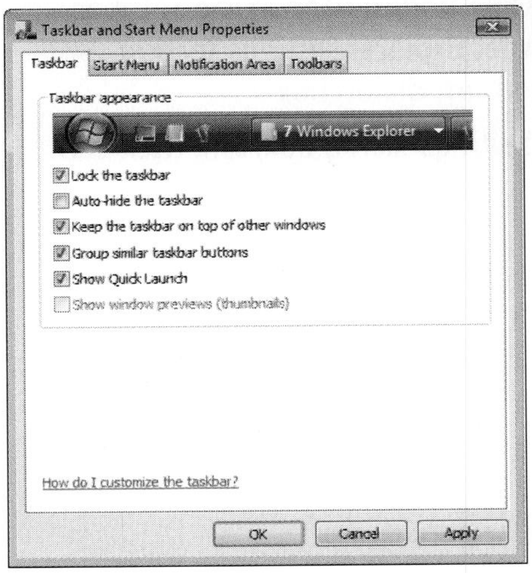

FIGURE A-3

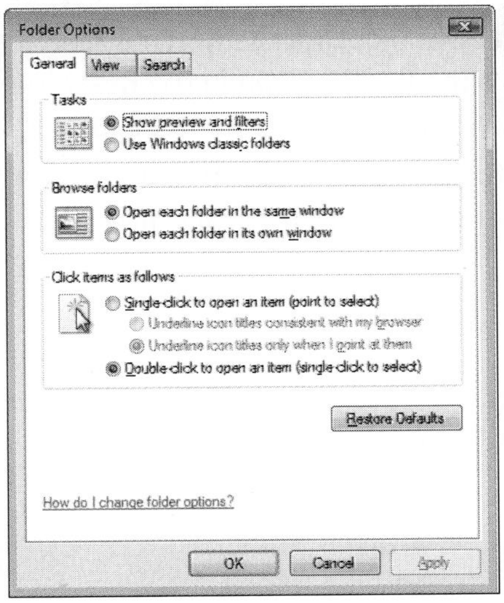

FIGURE A-4

FIGURE A-2

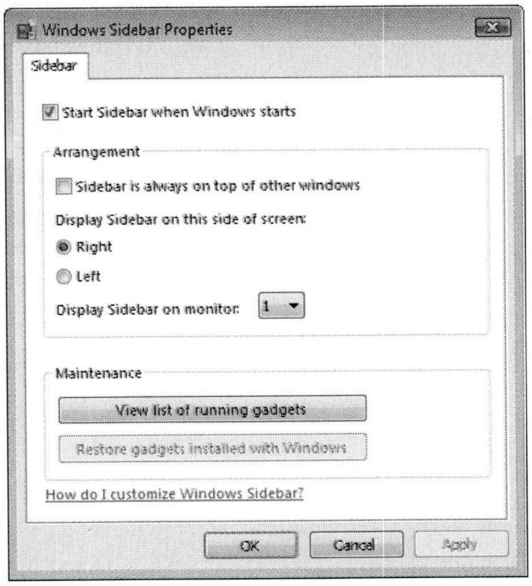

Restoring the Defaults in the Security Section

The following instructions require a default Windows Vista Ultimate installation and the student logged in with an Administrator account. All of the following settings can be changed by accessing the Control Panel.

STEPS

- **To restore the defaults in the Windows Firewall section**

  1. Click Start, and then click Control Panel. Click Security, click Windows Firewall, and then compare your screen to Figure A-5

  2. In the Windows Firewall dialog box, click Change settings. If the User Account Control dialog box appears, click Continue

  3. In the Windows Firewall Settings dialog box, click the Advanced tab. Click Restore Defaults, then click Yes in the Restore Defaults Confirmation dialog box

  4. Click OK to close the Windows Firewall Settings dialog box, and then close the Windows Firewall window

- **To restore the defaults in the Internet Options section**

  1. Click Start, and then click Control Panel. Click Security, click Internet Options, and then compare your screen to Figure A-6

  2. In the Internet Properties dialog box, on the General tab, click the Use default button. Click the Settings button in the Tabs section, and then click the Restore defaults button in the Tabbed Browsing Settings dialog box. Click OK to close the Tabbed Browsing Settings dialog box

  3. On the Security tab of the Internet Properties dialog box, click to uncheck the Enable Protected Mode checkbox, if necessary. Click the Default level button in the Security level for this zone section. If possible, click the Reset all zones to default level button

  4. On the Programs tab, click the Make default button in the Default web browser button for Internet Explorer, if possible. If Office is installed, Microsoft Office Word should be selected in the HTML editor drop-down list

  5. On the Advanced tab, click the Restore advanced settings button in the Settings section. Click the Reset button in the Reset Internet Explorer settings section, and then click Reset in the Reset Internet Explorer Settings dialog box

  6. Click Close to close the Reset Internet Explorer Settings dialog box, and then click OK to close the Internet Properties dialog box

FIGURE A-5

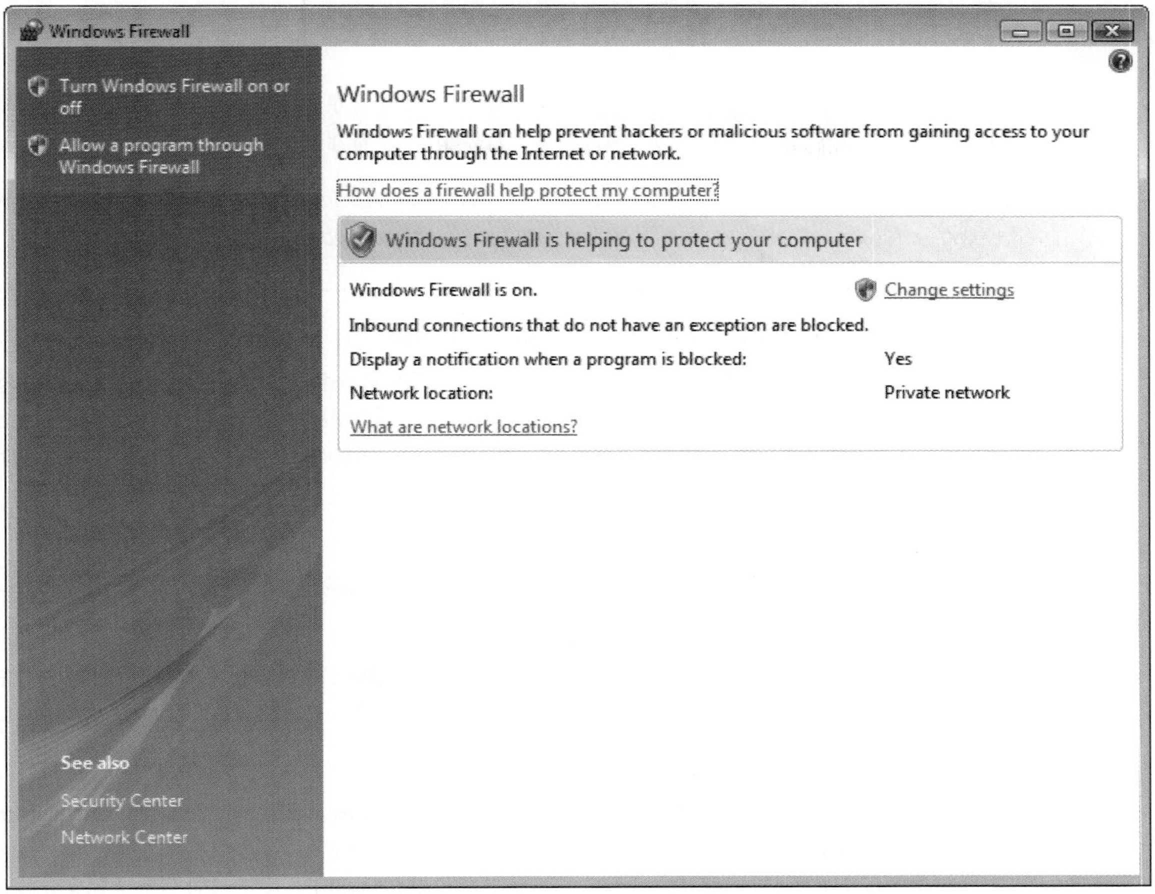

FIGURE A-6

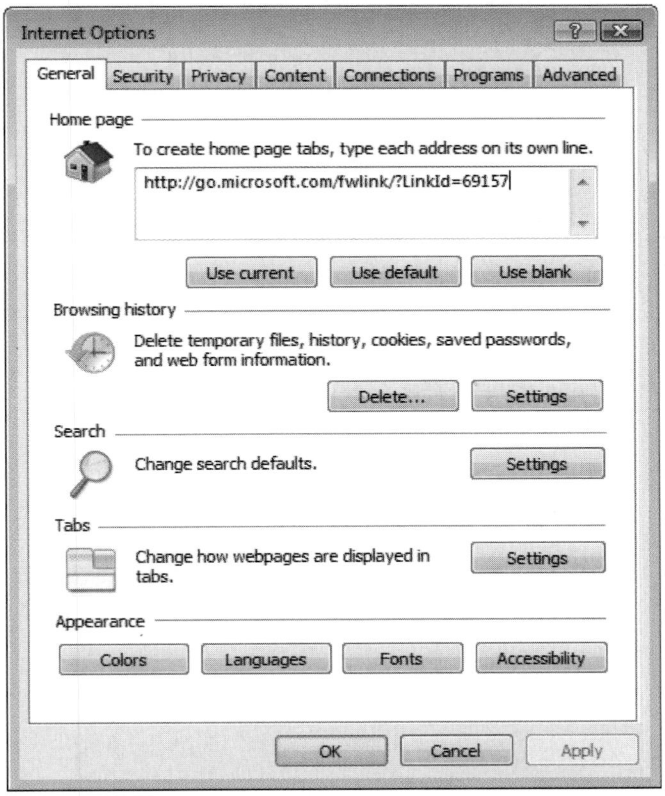

Restoring the Defaults in the Hardware and Sound Section

The following instructions require a default Windows Vista Ultimate installation and the student logged in with an Administrator account. All of the following settings can be changed by accessing the Control Panel.

STEPS

- To restore the defaults in the Autoplay section
    1. Click Start, and then click Control Panel. Click Hardware and Sound, click Autoplay, and then compare your screen to Figure A-7. Scroll down and click the Reset all defaults button in the Devices section at the bottom of the window, and then click Save

- To restore the defaults in the Sound section
    1. Click Start, and then click Control Panel. Click Hardware and Sound, click Sound, and then compare your screen to Figure A-8
    2. In the Sound dialog box, on the Sounds tab, select Windows Default from the Sound Scheme drop-down list, and then click OK

- To restore the defaults in the Mouse section
    1. Click Start, and then click Control Panel. Click Hardware and Sound, click Mouse, and then compare your screen to Figure A-9
    2. In the Mouse Properties dialog box, on the Pointers tab, select Windows Aero (system scheme) from the Scheme drop-down list
    3. Click OK to close the Mouse Properties dialog box

FIGURE A-7

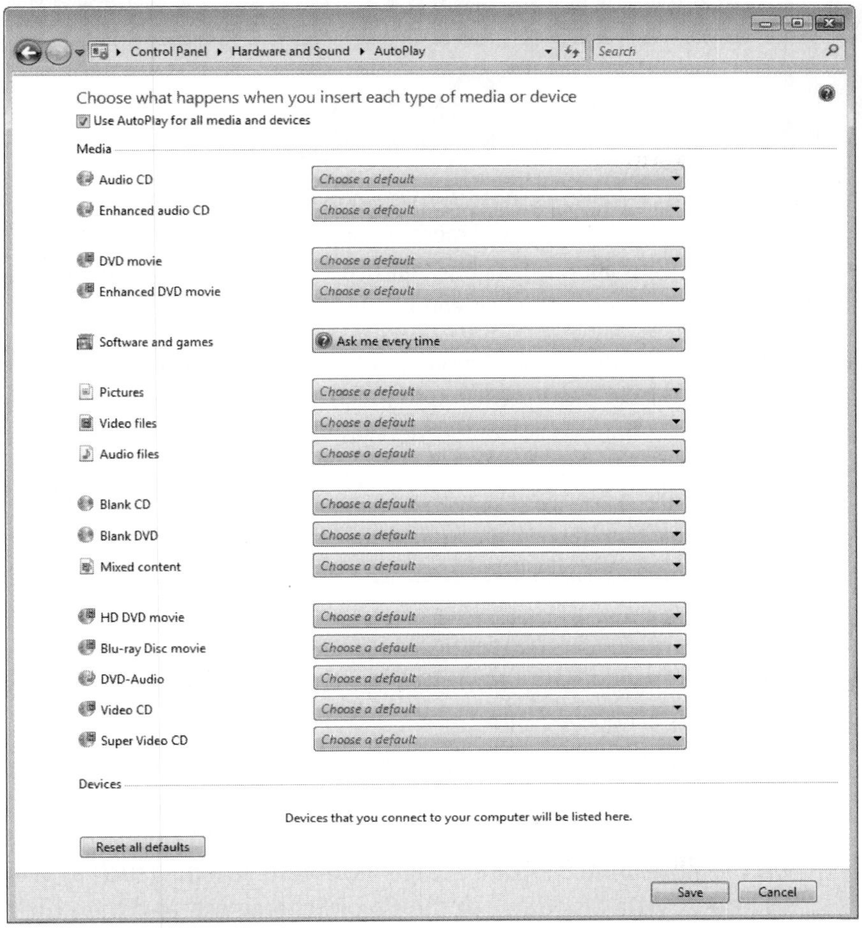

Control Panel ▸ Hardware and Sound ▸ AutoPlay | Search

Choose what happens when you insert each type of media or device

☑ Use AutoPlay for all media and devices

Media

Audio CD — Choose a default ▾

Enhanced audio CD — Choose a default ▾

DVD movie — Choose a default ▾

Enhanced DVD movie — Choose a default ▾

Software and games — Ask me every time ▾

Pictures — Choose a default ▾

Video files — Choose a default ▾

Audio files — Choose a default ▾

Blank CD — Choose a default ▾

Blank DVD — Choose a default ▾

Mixed content — Choose a default ▾

HD DVD movie — Choose a default ▾

Blu-ray Disc movie — Choose a default ▾

DVD-Audio — Choose a default ▾

Video CD — Choose a default ▾

Super Video CD — Choose a default ▾

Devices

Devices that you connect to your computer will be listed here.

Reset all defaults

Save   Cancel

FIGURE A-8

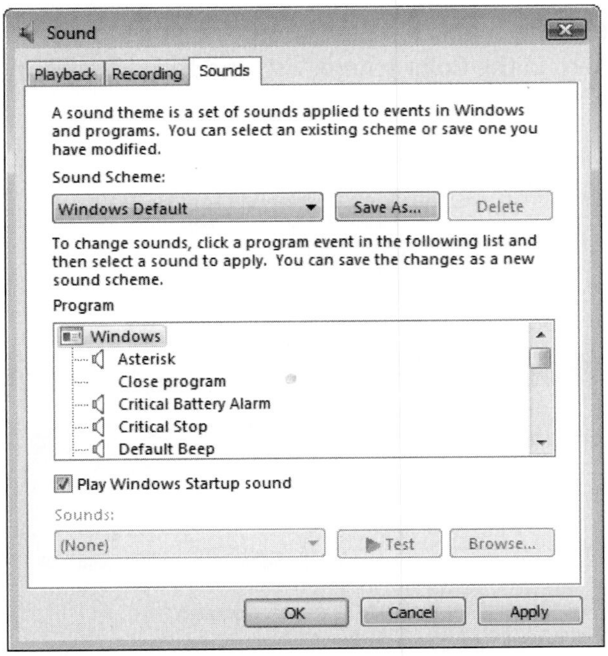

Sound

Playback | Recording | Sounds

A sound theme is a set of sounds applied to events in Windows and programs. You can select an existing scheme or save one you have modified.

Sound Scheme:

Windows Default ▾   Save As...   Delete

To change sounds, click a program event in the following list and then select a sound to apply. You can save the changes as a new sound scheme.

Program

☐ Windows
  ◻ Asterisk
  ◻ Close program
  ◻ Critical Battery Alarm
  ◻ Critical Stop
  ◻ Default Beep

☑ Play Windows Startup sound

Sounds:

(None) ▾   ▶ Test   Browse...

OK   Cancel   Apply

FIGURE A-9

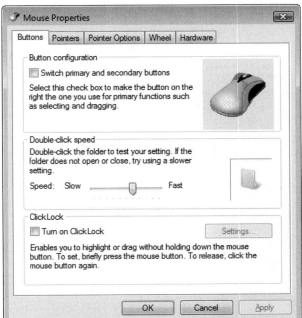

Mouse Properties

Buttons | Pointers | Pointer Options | Wheel | Hardware

Button configuration

☐ Switch primary and secondary buttons

Select this check box to make the button on the right the one you use for primary functions such as selecting and dragging.

Double-click speed

Double-click the folder to test your setting. If the folder does not open or close, try using a slower setting.

Speed: Slow ——————◻—— Fast

ClickLock

☐ Turn on ClickLock   Settings...

Enables you to highlight or drag without holding down the mouse button. To set, briefly press the mouse button. To release, click the mouse button again.

OK   Cancel   Apply

Disabling and Enabling Windows Aero

Unlike prior versions of Windows, Windows Vista provides two distinct user interface experiences: a "basic" experience for entry-level systems and more visually dynamic experience called Windows Aero. Both offer a new and intutive navgation experience that helps you more easily find and organize your applications and files, but Aero goes further by delivering a truly next-generation desktop experience.

Windows Aero builds on the basic Windows Vista user experience and offers Mircosoft's best-designed, highest-preforming desktop experience. Using Aero requires a PC with compatible graphics adapter and running a Premium or Business edition of Windows Vista.

The following instructions require a computer capable of running Windows Aero, with a default Windows Vista Ultimate installation and student logged in with an Administrator account.

STEPS

- **To Disable Windows Aero**

  We recommend that students using this book disable Windows Aero and restore their operating systems default settings (instructions to follow).

  1. **Right-click the desktop, select Personalize, and then compare yor screen in Figure A-10. Select Window Color and Appearance, and then select Open classic appeareance properties for more color options. In Appearance Settings dialong box, on the Appearance tab, select any non-Aero scheme (such as Windows Vista Basic or Windows Vista Standard) in the Color Scheme list, and then click OK Figure A-11 compares Windows Aero to other color schemes. Note that this book uses Windows Vista Basic as the color scheme**

- **To Enable Windows Aero**

  1. **Right-click the desktop, and then select Personalize. Select Window Color and Appearance, then select Windows Aero in the Color scheme list, and then click OK in the Appearance Settings dialog box**

FIGURE A-10   FIGURE A-11

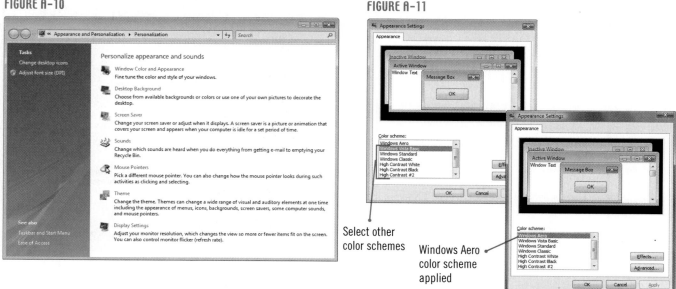

Select other color schemes

Windows Aero color scheme applied

Glossary

Active The currently available document, program, or object; on the taskbar, the button of the active document appears in a darker shade while the buttons of other open documents are dimmed.

Appointment In the Calendar in Outlook, an activity that does not involve inviting other people or scheduling resources.

Attachment A file, such as a picture, audio clip, video clip, document, worksheet, or presentation, that is sent in addition to the e-mail message composed by typing in the Message window.

Backward-compatible Software feature that enables documents saved in an older version of a program to be opened in a newer version of the program.

Blind courtesy copy (BCC) In e-mail, a way to send a message to a recipient who needs to be aware of the correspondence between the sender and the recipients, but is not the primary recipient of the message, and is used when the sender does not want to reveal who has received courtesy copies.

Calendar In Microsoft Outlook, provides a convenient way to manage your appointments and events.

Categories In Outlook, a feature used to tag items so you can track and organize them by specific criteria.

Clipboard Temporary storage area in Windows.

Compatible The capability of different programs to work together and exchange data.

Computer network The hardware and software that make it possible for two or more computers to share information and resources.

Contacts In Microsoft Outlook, enables you to manage all your business and personal contact information.

Contextual tab Tab on the Ribbon that appears when needed to complete a specific task; for example, if you select a chart in an Excel workbook, three contextual Chart Tool tabs (Design, Layout, and Format) appear.

Courtesy copy (CC) In e-mail, a way to send a message to a recipient who needs to be aware of the correspondence between the sender and the recipients, but is not the primary recipient of the message.

Date Navigator A monthly calendar in the To-Do Bar that gives you an overview of the month.

Deleted Items folder The folder that stores items when you delete or erase a message from any mail folder, rather than being immediately, permanently deleted. Also called Trash folder.

Dialog box launcher An icon available in many groups on the Ribbon that you can click to open a dialog box or task pane, offering an alternative way to choose commands.

Distribution list A collection of contacts to whom you want to send the same messages; makes it possible for you to send a message to the same group without having to select each contact in the group.

Document window Workspace in the program window that displays the current document.

Electronic mail (e-mail) The technology that makes it possible for you to send and receive messages through the Internet.

E-mail message The message sent using e-mail technology.

E-mail software Enables you to send and receive e-mail messages over a network, within an intranet, and through the Internet.

Event In the Calendar in Outlook, an activity that lasts 24 hours or longer.

File An electronic collection of stored data that has a unique name, distinguishing it from other files.

Filter Used to create a subset of a list, you search for only specific information—for example, in Outlook Contacts, filter only for those contacts who live in New Jersey.

Forwarding Sending an e-mail message you have received to someone else.

Gallery A collection of choices you can browse through to make a selection. Often available with Live Preview.

Group On the Ribbon, a set of related commands on a tab.

Inbox A mail folder that stores all incoming mail.

Integrate To incorporate a document and parts of a document created in one program into another program; for example, to incorporate an Excel chart into a PowerPoint slide, or an Access table into a Word document.

Interface The look and feel of a program; for example, the appearance of commands and the way they are organized in the program window.

Internet A network of connected computers and computer networks located around the world.

Intranet A computer network that connects computers in a local area only, such as computers in a company's office.

Journal In Outlook, provides a trail of your activities within Microsoft Office by tracking all documents, spreadsheets, databases, presentations, or any Office file that you specify. When turned on, you can see a timeline of any calls, messages, appointments, or tasks.

Junk e-mail Unwanted mail that arrives from unsolicited sources. Also called spam.

Launch To open or start a program on your computer.

Live Preview A feature that lets you point to a choice in a gallery or palette and see the results in the document without actually clicking the choice.

Meeting In the Calendar in Outlook, an activity you invite people to or reserve resources for.

Message body In an e-mail message, where you write the text of your message.

Message header Contains the basic information about a message including the sender's name and e-mail address, the names and e-mail addresses of recipients and CC recipients, a date and time stamp, and the subject of the message.

Navigation Pane In Outlook in Normal view, it is typically on the left side of the screen, showing you the folder list in addition to the navigation shortcuts.

Notes In Outlook, the electronic version of the sticky notes or Post-It™ notes you buy at your local stationery store; a convenient way to quickly jot down a reminder or an idea.

Online collaboration The ability to incorporate feedback or share information across the Internet or a company network or intranet.

Outbox A temporary storage folder for e-mail messages that have not yet been sent.

Outlook Today Shows your day at a glance, like an electronic version of a daily planner book. When it is open, you can see what is happening in the Calendar, Tasks, and Messages for the day.

Personal account In Outlook, identifies you as a user with information such as your e-mail address and password, the type of Internet service provider (ISP) you are using, and the incoming and outgoing mail server address for your ISP.

Previewing Prior to printing, to see onscreen exactly how the printed document will look.

Program tab Single tab on the Ribbon specific to a particular view, such as Print Preview.

Quick Access toolbar Customizable toolbar that includes buttons for common Office commands, such as saving a file and undoing an action.

Really Simple Syndication (RSS) A format for feeding or syndicating news or any content from Web sites to your computer.

Ribbon Area that displays commands for the current Office program, organized into tabs and groups.

Rule When using Outlook, enables you to organize your mail, by setting parameters for incoming mail. For example, you can specify that all mail from a certain person goes into the folder for a specific project.

Screen capture A snapshot of your screen, as if you took a picture of it with a camera, which you can paste into a document.

Sent Items folder When you send an e-mail message, a copy of the message is stored in this folder to help you track the messages you send out.

Service provider The organization or company that provides e-mail or Internet access.

Spam Unwanted mail that arrives from unsolicited sources. Also called junk e-mail.

Spamming The sending of identical or near-identical unsolicited messages to a large number of recipients. Many e-mail programs have filters that identify this mail and place it in a special folder.

Store-and-forward technology Messages are *stored* on a service provider's computer until a recipient logs on to a computer and requests his or her messages. At that time, the messages are *forwarded* to the recipient's computer.

Suite A group of programs that are bundled together and share a similar interface, making it easy to transfer skills and program content among them.

Tab A set of commands on the Ribbon related to a common set of tasks or features. Tabs are further organized into groups of related commands.

Tasks In Outlook, the electronic to-do list, whereby each task has a subject, a start and end date, priority, and a description.

Themes Predesigned combinations of colors, fonts, and formatting attributes you can apply to a document in any Office program.

Title bar Area at the top of every program window that displays the document and program name.

Username The first part of an e-mail address that identifies the person who receives the mail that is sent to this e-mail address.

User interface A collective term for all the ways you interact with a software program.

VCards The Internet standard for creating and sharing virtual business cards.

Views Display settings that show or hide selected elements of a document in the document window, to make it easier to focus on a certain task, such as formatting or reading text.

Zooming in A feature that makes a document appear bigger but shows less of it onscreen at once; does not affect actual document size.

Zooming out A feature that shows more of a document onscreen at once but at a reduced size; does not affect actual document size.

Index

courtesy copies, OUT 6
creating messages, OUT 6, OUT 7
distribution lists, OUT 16
flagging messages, OUT 13
folders, OUT 8–9
forwarding messages, OUT 12–13
good practices, OUT 16–17
labeling messages, OUT 13
message content, OUT 3
message headers, OUT 7, OUT 8, OUT 9
message options, OUT 15
messages, OUT 2, OUT 3
organizing, OUT 28–29
privacy, OUT 3
receiving messages, OUT 10, OUT 11
replying to messages, OUT 10, OUT 11
sending messages, OUT 6, OUT 7
shortcuts, OUT 17
software, OUT 2
sorting, OUT 9
uses, OUT 2
vacation responses, OUT 11
Web-based, OUT 5, OUT 10
e-mail addresses
formats, OUT 5
multiple, sending to, OUT 6
parts, OUT 4
e-mail programs, starting, OUT 6
e-mail providers, OUT 4, OUT 5
emoticons, OUT 17
errors. *See* correcting errors
events, Calendar, OUT 32
Excel, OFF 2, OFF 3. *See also* chart(s); worksheet(s)
exiting
programs, OFF 4, OFF 5

►F

file(s)
attaching to e-mails, OUT 14–15
creating, OFF 8, OFF 9
.docx, OFF 8
opening, OFF 10, OFF 11
.pptx, OFF 8
recovering, OFF 15
saving, OFF 8, OFF 9, OFF 10, OFF 11
file extensions, Office programs, OFF 8

filenames
Office programs, OFF 8
filtering
mailing lists, OUT 31
flagging e-mail messages, OUT 13
forwarding e-mail messages, OUT 12–13

►G

group(s)
commands, OFF 6
e-mail distribution lists, OUT 16

►H

header(s)
e-mail messages, OUT 7, OUT 8, OUT 9
Help system, OFF 14–15. *See also* Windows Help and Support

►I

Inbox, OUT 8, OUT 9
integration, OFF 2
interface(s), OFF 2
Internet, OUT 2
intranets, OUT 2

►J

Journal, OUT 38–39
Journal Options dialog box, OUT 38, OUT 39
jump drives. *See* USB flash drives
Junk E-mail folder, OUT 8, OUT 9
Junk E-mail Options dialog box, OUT 28, OUT 29

►K

keychain drives. *See* USB flash drives

►L

labeling e-mail messages, OUT 13
launching programs, OFF 4, OFF 5
Live Preview feature, OFF 6

►M

mailing lists, OUT 31
filtering, OUT 31
meetings, Calendar, OUT 32
Message Options dialog box, OUT 15
multiple e-mail addresses, sending to, OUT 6

►T

tab(s)
  contextual, OFF 6
  program windows, OFF 7
Tasks, OUT 34–35
title bar
  program windows, OFF 6, OFF 7
To-Do Bar, Outlook, OUT 26, OUT 27
tracking activities, OUT 38–39
tracking items, OUT 40–41
Trash folder, OUT 8, OUT 9

►U

Undo button, OFF 6
user interface, OFF 6–7
username, OUT 4

►V

vacation responses, e-mail, OUT 11

►W

Web-based e-mail, OUT 5, OUT 10
Word, OFF 2, OFF 3. *See also* document(s); text
workbooks
  file extension, OFF 8

►X

.xisx file extension, OFF 8

►Z

Zoom button, OFF 12, OFF 13
Zoom slider
  program windows, OFF 7
zooming in, OFF 12, OFF 13
zooming out, OFF 12, OFF 13